THE
SPIRIT STILLS
THE
STORMS

THE
SPIRIT STILLS
THE
STORMS

From Tyranny to the American Dream

"SAM" LIEN LE

To: SALLY & CHARLES

7-25-13

Thank you,
Please enjoy
and
be inspired.

Sam

Published by Tate Publishing & Enterprises, LLC
127 E. Trade Center Terrace | Mustang, Oklahoma 73064 USA
1.888.361.9473 | www.tatepublishing.com

Tate Publishing is committed to excellence in the publishing industry. The company reflects the philosophy established by the founders, based on Psalm 68:11,
"The Lord gave the word and great was the company of those who published it."

Published in the United States of America

ISBN: 978-1-61566-830-4
1. Biography & Autobiography / Personal Memoirs
2. Biography & Autobiography / Historical
10.01.25

ACKNOWLEDGMENTS

I wish to thank my wife my children and grandchildren, for whom this book is written. Without their love and support, this book would not have been possible.

My very special thanks to Ray Striler, who said, "Sam, you are king of storytellers. Go finish it on paper." That did it!

Ann Bjorklund, I am forever indebted to you. You worked tirelessly editing my book and said it was your love. Thank you.

I would also like to thank Marvin Carr, Marlene and Ed Morrow, Annie Nichols, Steve Cordahl, Martin Springer, Mai-Phuong Nguyen, Vu Huynh, Linda and Jim Hunt, and Franklin Duncan. Your encouragement has become my elixir, my impetus, from the conception of my book to its birth. I gratefully bow my head to you all and say thank you.

And for those who have touched me with your kind words but are not acknowledged here, please accept my deep appreciation.

AUTHOR'S NOTE

This is a work of nonfiction; I have used real names with the exception of Mr. Hoang. The pseudonym is used at his request because of political sensitivities in the People's Republic of Vietnam.

I have told this true story to my dear friends and now recently to my close family. They all said, "Write it. You tell it so well. It comes to life when you put it into words."

So here is my attempt to tell you my incredible journey that was undoubtedly guided by a spirit.

The experience was there, so true and magnificently, exquisitely beautiful, even though coated with tears and heartbreak. I, at times, wrestled with ideas of how to bring this picture, this experience to life, so that you as a reader could see what I saw and feel what I felt. I was debating whether I should use my second language, English, or my native tongue, Vietnamese, to write the story. Obviously, you see my choice.

Back in the sixties, or to be exact, somewhere in the summer of 1966, barely at the age of nineteen, freshly out of high school, I decided to join the US Special Forces as a combat interpreter.

"What is the difference between the single-shot rifle, carbine, and the automatic machine gun?" It was the only question posed to me by an operations officer at the B-23 in Ban-Me-Thuot before I was accepted to join with the brave Green Berets. It was a question of my fate, and to be able to answer it correctly in English determined my fate as well.

I was born in North Vietnam at the end of 1946 on December 21, in Sontay province about thirty-five miles north of Hanoi. When the French military was utterly defeated at Dien-Bien-phu battle in 1954, the whole country was divided in two parts, North and South, politically and geographically, at the 17th parallel as stipulated by the Geneva Conference. My parents and I were among hundedreds of thousands Vietnamese, fled from the communists to South Vietnam, creating the biggest exodus of refugees in the history of Vietnam.

And like many youngsters, I was taught French in grade school. English was not an option for me until high school. I am forever grateful to my English teacher, Mr. Thong, and his good-looking American friend, a US combat pilot who would come to my English class for vocal drills once a week. That is the secret to how I picked up my American English accent.

I hope that I have confessed enough about my English acquiring background, and here is the test for me to convey to you my true story of my journey to the promised land of America.

If this book touches you in any way, then I, in my humble way, have succeeded with my choice.

My heartfelt thanks to you, and may the spirit which stills the storms be with you.

—"Sam" Lien Le

A chickpea leaps almost over the rim of the pot where it's being boiled.

"Why are you doing this to me?"

The cook knocks him down with the ladle.

"Don't you try to jump out. You think I'm torturing you? I'm giving you flavor so you can mix with spices and rice and be the lovely vitality of a human being. Remember when you drank rain in the garden? That was for this."

—"Chickpea to Cook" by Jelaluddin Rumi

TABLE OF CONTENTS

INTRODUCTION

I first met the remarkable author of *The Spirit Stills the Storms* through visits to his successful and creative home furnishings and silk flower store in Spokane. As I have always been interested in immigrant stories, we began a conversation and then a friendship, which gradually gave me a picture of the fierce determination behind his courteous and gentle demeanor. As I learned more of the dramatic details behind Lien Le and his family's escape plans, their dangerous dash out to the South China Sea, their near miracle survival through a typhoon, and finally his leadership in a refugee camp, his seemed to be a story that deserved to become a part of our nation's history.

Like many other Americans, I recall seeing photographs of daring Vietnamese boat people who risked their lives seeking freedom after the Communist takeover at the end of the war. Who were these fathers, mothers, and children riding the high sea in flimsy, overcrowded boats, risking both capture or drowning in search of a new life? Our nation's story is inextricably bound to their personal stories, but we know so little. Often the immigrant story stays silent; even their own children know little of what motivated such significant upheaval and great loss, which provided new opportunities for their families.

To help fill this historical gap, Lien Le offers his story with immense detail of the courage, tenacity, creativity, and cunning that it took to reach his goal of giving his children a chance for freedom. Born in humble conditions, bereft from the death of his mother when he was barely seven years of age, but possessing exceptional character and fortitude, he joined the Special Forces during the Vietnam War as a teenager, married and became the father of two young sons, and endured imprisonment after the collapse of the South Vietnam. For years, he plotted and planned his audacious quest for freedom from tyranny.

This glimpse into the soul of Lien Le shows his innate capacity to cherish life. Whether describing his awe over nature's beauty during meditative moments on the Camranh Bay, reflecting on protection during numerous near-death experiences that enhanced his sense of faith in a great spirit, or sharing life wisdom on our human need to forgive, dream, and risk, his vibrant memory and gifts as a storyteller are a treasure to the reader. In many ways, his life seems to illustrate the insights of Victor Frank, author of *Man's Search for Meaning*, who lived through the Holocaust in concentration camps and observed, "Everything can be taken from a man but one thing; the last of the human freedoms—to choose one's attitude in any given set of circumstances, to choose one's own way."

I hope you will savor the story of how Lien Le chose his own way and dared to follow his dreams. His life choices offered opportunities for all of his family members, but his choices have also affected the Spokane community and our country, which gain immensely because we have his presence as part of our heritage. Enjoy!

—Linda Lawrence Hunt, author of *Bold Spirit: Helga Estby's Forgotten Walk Across Victorian America*

ESCAPE INTO THE UNKNOWN

The last person was pulled onto the boat. All commotion suddenly died out, and the engine roared alive. The boat, at full speed, left the mouth of Cam Ranh Bay, heading east into the unknown waters of the high seas.

It was 2:00 a.m. on October 12, 1979. Here and there hundreds of tiny lights of night fishing boats danced and twinkled in the morning hours. *How many of them,* I wondered, *are patrol boats?* There was no time to worry now; the best one could do at this moment was to avoid coming close to any of the lights. Any of the boats could be a patrol boat. The chance of getting caught out here, outside the mouth of the bay, was unlikely, but one could never be sure.

Only a couple of hours ago everyone was on the two little taxi boats: one hauling fuel and supplies and the other, escapees. We all passed by the security watchtower under the crescent moonlight, making everything on the boat even more visible. We were vulnerable. A few of our men scurried around a stack of ruffled fishing nets, pretending to be busy with preparation for a fishing trip. Our calculation, based on inside tips and information, was that early morning hours were the best for us because this was when hundreds of fishing boats started their day and the patrols reduced their activities.

As our little taxi boat passed by the security post, which was situated above the cliff, we were holding our breath, praying that the guard would not notice any abnormality about our boat. Perhaps our boat was a little heavier than normal. Or better yet, we were hoping that all the guards would have fallen asleep on their watch. It was about between 1 and 1:30 a.m., which was about half an hour before we took off from the mouth of Cam Ranh Bay heading towards the high sea.

I was transported by a taxi boat from the beach to the bigger boat anchored at the mouth of the bay. Our prayers were answered and our hope was still alive, for now we were on the bigger boat, a fishing boat, mingling among hundreds of others, and I wondered how many of them out there were heading to the international waters and having no plans to return to their homeland.

The monotony of the diesel engine, the relief from fear of getting caught, and most of all, the exhaustion had helped everyone ease into their sleeping. I was too tired to fall asleep; my eyes were burning with discomfort due to stress and many nights without rest.

I was led onto a taxi boat from the hideout in Xuan Ninh, a village near the beach of Cam Ranh Bay. There my wife, her brother and sister, and my two sons were among many escapees hiding in different houses. I hoped they were now on the other taxi boat, safe and sound heading out to the mouth of Cam Ranh Bay to join me on the bigger boat. As I climbed onboard the boat, I noticed there were many people onboard already, almost all of whom I had never met or known, but who had the very same desire to get out. I came to realize the gravity of the situation. If we did not take off soon, we would all be caught by the local guards. However, if we left with a load of this many people, we would not go very far before we all sank into the water, just like many others whose boats were overloaded. I knew I had to act now and act quickly. I told a few youngsters who were sitting next to me that they needed to get off the boat. They were not paid passengers. They just sat there motionless like sculptures and said nothing, as if I were talking to stones or to lifeless persons. They pretended they did not hear me. After explaining to them the dangers and other uncertainties, I found out that my persuasion was utterly fruitless and that I would have to push them off the boat. My God! There were quite a few of them! I then came to a scary realization that the situation of them versus me would be reversed if they united. They could force me into their position; they could tie me up and roll me off the boat, waving me a good-bye. It had happened in the past in this coastal area where there were a few incidents of boat pirating. The boat owners were under gunpoint to get off the boat or forced to come along.

After all, we had no time to waste, and no other choice but to take off with whatever and whoever was on the boat. Here I was now, on this bigger boat, seeing lots of strangers lying and sitting in every corner of the boat. Just an hour ago in the dark, when the passengers boarded and identified themselves and named their sponsor, they all responded with "Mr. Le." I did not give them that authority, but someone did and probably made lots of money in so doing.

Now I understood what had happened. I was seeing the whole process. The operators of the taxi boats had sold far too many seats to these strangers for gold or cash or other prearranged forms of payment and gave my name to be their sponsor if anyone asked. Fifty or sixty plus extra people would bring these operators lots of money, lots of gold, and they would become very rich overnight. They could care less about the safety or the welfare of those whom they had added to the load. The boat owner seemed quite upset at the fact that there were a lot more people than we had planned for this trip. He must have suspected me of wrongdoing since all the strangers, unbeknownst to me, gave my name. The agreement among our circle of friends was to have no more than thirty-five people, and here, at the first glance, one could tell the number was at least seventy, eighty, or even one hundred. There were more to be counted, for there were some who were hiding in some dark corners of the boat. The only way I could get myself out of this mess, this misunderstanding, was to ask these not-too-familiar faces how and what got them here on this boat. But they were all seasick; they looked shabby and very unhealthy. Some had already begun throwing up. Others wet their pants. There were no toilets on this fishing boat, and the odor of this combination was getting quite strong. I might have to wait for an appropriate time to get to the bottom of this matter. I wanted to get a full explanation from these people as to who they were and how they got on this boat so that the boat owner would not think that I was doing something unethical or making money at his expense.

By daybreak, the stretch of mountains in the back of Cam Ranh Bay had almost faded away into the sky. In front of us, to the other end of the sea, the pinkish dawn of morning sun was beginning to rise, promising a clear, beautiful day. It had been about four hours since we started heading out, and I had no idea how far we had travelled or whereabout we were at this point. We were pretty sure we had left all other fishing boats behind, and from here on, we just had to do our best to avoid any passing vessels. We did not want to be picked up or escorted back to Cam Ranh Bay area by a Russian ship. The government of Socialist Vietnam had an agreement with the Russians to return refugees back to Vietnam. Our estimation was that it would take us four to five days to get to the Philippine shorelines under ideal weather conditions. However, wouldn't it also be much nicer if we were all, by our good fortune, picked up by some commercial fishing vessel or some US navy ship that might happen to be in the vicinity? Now nearly everyone was exhausted but in high spirits because we were no longer in danger of being caught, handcuffed, and taken back to the inland.

The boat remained at a fairly good speed, cutting through the morning calm surface of the water. Here and there a few flying fish raced along our boat, and every now and then, they dashed themselves off the water and into the air as if they were sharing our moments of joy. As they swam alongside the boat, they seemed to be a symbol of the freedom we felt. As we were farther out into the sea, I was looking for a deeper dark blue water, as I was once told by some fishermen that the way to tell whether you are on the international waters is to look at the color of the water. But the color had not changed as I had observed; maybe I was not out there yet, or maybe they were just kidding. It was just a beautiful day with blue skies; a few thin clumps of white cloud floated above like stretches of loose cotton. I was expecting a warm day ahead; maybe some of us could have a dip into the sea when it got really warm. I was just daydreaming and dozing off, thinking of an eventful night, the night at the beach house.

Not too long after I was in my little nap, I was awakened by a commotion on the boat. The boat captain had spotted an incoming ship, and people were whispering about what should be done. Some showed excitement while others seemed anxious. A decision had to be made whether to approach the boat or avoid it entirely. It was a hard decision to make. The idea of getting aboard the ship and being taken to the shores of free-world countries was the greatest desire of everyone on this boat. And to continue our course straight to the Philippines had its own risks; who could tell the weather of tomorrow? Would this little fishing craft withstand the turmoil of the sea? Would it withstand the lousy stormy weather?

But the risk of being brought back to the inland had more impact on us than anything else. Therefore, our boat changed its course to avoid the ship, and I felt very comfortable with the decision. Some other people were not happy and voiced their opinion that it might be a friendly ship and avoiding it could be a big mistake.

It was such a beautiful day—the sky was blue, the sea was flat and round. There was hardly any sign of trouble with the weather, so why not keep on going? I myself had had enough trouble with the Communist government and would not take any chances, especially while I was enjoying the beginning of my freedom. I could never forget the faces of those guards at the prison in the Cam Ranh Bay area. They were mean spirited and heartless. The death penalty was waiting for me if I was ever again caught escaping. They had warned me! My choice was very clear, and so was my determination.

It was determined that we would continue easterly, despite the wind change that occurred while I was at the hideout in the village. My friend told me that the wind had changed its course from south to north. It meant the calm season was over for the South China Sea, and heading out into the sea to the Philippines could be very risky or suicidal. But my answer to that was, "My friend, we have come this far. We will not quit because the wind just changed its direction hours ago. So don't be afraid, and go on with the plan."

ESCAPE LONG AGO

I remember my very first escape with my family from North to South Vietnam in 1954 when I was only seven years of age. My father, a simple fisherman from a very small village of Son Tay province, was prosecuted by my uncle, my father's youngest brother, who had served in the French paratroops. When the French military was defeated at the Dien Bien Phu battle, my uncle Thu surrendered to the communists of Vietminh. In order to prove his loyalty to the Communists and to demonstrate his ability to do anything to earn trust from the new master, he had to set up a charge for the prosecution. What was the charge? I would never know, for I was too little to understand or to remember. As the trial was postponed to the following night, the next morning, even before dawn, my father, pretending to mend the bamboo roof for his fishing boat at the front yard of our house, was waiting for the right moment to get out of the village. Just as I was getting up from my sleep and walking toward him, he grabbed my hand, and we both vanished into the darkness of the morning hours. We were on the quiet, empty trail behind the village for almost an hour before we were able to emerge onto the main road heading to the city. By noon we had entered into the market, mingling with many hundreds of people. We knew that we were safe there. It was just my dad and me. My mother had to stay behind to avoid the watchful eyes of local cops.

With such a relief from fear of being caught, my father treated himself to a bowl of hot green tea from a tea peddler nearby, and my father and I hopped onto an electric car, which headed to Haiphong airfield. Upon our arrival, I was surprised and thrilled to see a friend's family from our village staying outside a long, metal building. I was too young to have the vaguest idea what was happening or to ask how and when they had arrived there ahead of us. The adults must have had their own plans that we as kids were not supposed to know, especially the runaway escape plan that they obviously had.

We cooked, slept, and waited along the wall outside of the building for almost a week, until one morning my father told me that if my mother did not show up, we would have to leave without her. It was supposed to be the very last flight to bring escapees, or refugees, from North to South Vietnam. Alas! It was the very last hour, the hour of decision-making, when my father had to choose whether to go or not to go with or without my mother and my little sister. I could feel the pain and tension on his face. I could see the agony, the internal struggle of weighing the yes and the no. The yes to go could mean eternal separation, and the other could mean imprisonment, torture, and death. Neither choice was an easy one for my father, but he was the one who had to make that choice. The tension weighed down on him; the anxiety heightened as the clock was ticking and time was running away. Dad was moving back and forth at the end of the building. Sometimes he sat on the ground, lost into his own thinking; other times, in desperation, he came over to his friends for advice and for comfort, hoping for miracles to happen.

Some people among the group started gathering their belongings as a sign that the time for boarding was approaching. Very soon, one by one, they would march toward the airfield, and we, my father and I, might not be among them to get on that airplane, which was parked quietly and patiently waiting in the hot sun while my father and I were anxiously waiting for my mother and my sister to join us on this flight. Somehow the chances were getting slimmer and slimmer as minutes passed by and they were nowhere to be seen. I felt the eyes and the hearts of our companion friends on us as if they were saying, "Come with us; they will be all right," or "You all should stay and wait for your wife, your mother. They may be on their way here. Don't go; be patient." I did not want to go without my mom and my sister. I would rather stay and wait for them. The thought of never being able to see them again was too painful for me to absorb. But I had to follow my dad wherever he decided to go. Every now and then, we would all look out into the road with the hope that they would emerge from any direction, walking toward us. I thought that she had been given instructions by my dad on how to get to this place and that she would find us in time. I silently prayed that she would make it before it was too late. I knew that I would be crying very hard and would not want to walk in the aircraft without them.

At the last minute, when all hope seemed to have evaporated with the heat of the July sun in the northern part of Vietnam, when the farewell and tears were about to begin, my mother and my sister finally appeared at the end of the road, heading toward us. My mom, with one hand holding my sister, the other carrying her tiny cloth bag, swiftly walked toward us as we rushed out to meet them. It was just a moment of indescribable happiness of our reunion as I embraced both of them with my tiny, short arms. My tears of joy began to well up, and I cried out, "*Me oi* (Oh, Mom)!"

She held me tightly to her and said, "*Dung khoc nao, con trai, ai ma lai di khoc* (Now, do not cry; boys are not supposed to be soft with tears, so don't cry, son)."

With that said, she joined us, running toward the airstrip. The boarding was about to begin. We were the last ones to be helped onto the aircraft, which was a small-size airplane, a French military bird that held no more than twenty people. We were squeezed in with another family at the middle of the aircraft and felt comfortable that we were together as a whole family again. It was a good feeling and a big silent thank you to the French aircrew that were patient so that this moment of reunion could happen.

After about ten minutes or so in the air, an incident happened that scared the soul out of us. We all thought that we were going to crash, as the side door of the plane suddenly flipped open and the airplane somehow lost its balance in the air. My father again, without being asked, showed his courage by having one of his arms hold tight to the inside of the aircraft, and the other reached out to pull down the door. Was he scared? I don't know. But one thing I know for sure is that my father always took initiative, always was a pioneer, and always was willing to take risks. Within a few minutes, he had the door pulled down, and the copilot appeared from the cabin to help him put it in the locking position. Through an interpreter, a French teacher who happened to be on board along with his family, the copilot told us that someone must have accidentally touched a knob or a switch that triggered the mechanism to release the door to flip it open. It was a miracle that no one was sucked out of the airplane, especially the boy about my age who touched the switch to make the door open. He made sure that no one was to be near the door for the rest of our flight. I was so proud of my father, a simple fisherman on the water, but a hero on the air. His finger was bleeding a little after the incident. He must have pulled it down very hard that a part of the skin of his finger was scraped off. He was my hero! The flight continued south without further incidents, thank God.

After landing in the South, we stayed in a temporary holding refugee center for a week or so, and then he moved my family to Tay Ninh province to start a new life among the many other refugees.

Life was pretty rough there for the newcomers. My father teamed up with other adult men doing the logging for firewood. He would stack his firewood by the side of the road and sell it by the truckload to the people in the city. Not very long after our arrival, my mother had an infection after giving birth to my sister who died prematurely. Her infection got worse due to lack of medical care; antibiotics were completely out of reach for all of us in this part of the country. After a few months of fighting the illness, she lost her strength and went to heaven. In just less than a year, running away from my birthplace, I first lost my sister to a cold with high fever, and now my mother. I was now the only survivor of her children.

My father realized that life there was not for a fisherman like him and decided to move to the central highlands, where there was a river and the fish were ample. K'rong Ana was the name of the river where my childhood years were spent in very peaceful ways. A few kids my age would get together at night on a little boat anchored at the middle of the river, fishing and cooking throughout the night. Cricket fights were always fun and catching them, a challenge.

We would tiptoe, gingerly approaching in the direction of the singing cricket. We knew that any sounds, any noise, would cause him to stop singing, and his nest, or a tiny hole in the ground where he was hiding, would elude us and never be found. It was the male crickets that made the noise; we heard them in the morning, evening, and even at night. I remember being amazed that such a little critter could sing so loudly, not by his mouth, not by his internal organs, but by rubbing together his rugged wings. It was always soul soothing to litsen to the crickets singing in the evening or in the quiet of the night.

"Rice is ready," someone said, and I was awakened from my short nap to see a bowl of rice passed on to me from the back of the boat, where the boat captain and his wife had cooked some rice for his family and were nice enough to share. It dawned on me that I had not had a meal for the last few days. I was always on the go, always thinking how to execute the plan flawlessly, because if anything went wrong, death or the prison was waiting for me and for all of us on this boat. The food was quite tasty, despite the fact that I was at the point of exhaustion. It could have been because I saw the happy faces of my wife and my children, who were enjoying the first day of their journey. Maybe it was because I began to realize this was the beginning of my freedom I had been yearning for, or perhaps it was the combination of it all that added flavors to my rice. It was just a total relief from all anxiety and nervousness, which seemed to evaporate in such a nice day in the open sea, free from the government, free from the guards whose hands are like those of giant octopuses ready to wrap around you and to choke you to death. I could not help but think of the incident that happened only two days ago in the village where the boat owner was living.

The liaison person failed to deliver payment. I therefore took the bus from Cam Ranh Bay to the boat owner's house to pay him in gold so that he could give it to his parents who decided not to come along. As my guide, a little twelve-year-old girl took me into the house after a long walk from the bus station. Mr. Man, the boat owner, was very surprised to see me there. I could see his face suddenly change color and become worried as he told me that I should not have come to his house. But it was too late for us to say anything to each other because the two cops, the under-covers, the real cops, who had been watching him and his family, appeared at the door. I was a little shocked for a few seconds, realizing that I had been wearing the uniform of a Communist soldier, a pale khaki long-sleeved shirt and trousers, and on my feet, a pair of light, oak-colored strap sandals. This was how I could get around easier in town or to another city. But if I ever got caught, my life would be doomed! And here I was in a situation confronting the two real cops. Looking at me, one of them asked me, "Who are you? What are you doing here? Show me your ID."

Knowing that I had only seconds to act and to show them that I was just a real soldier as they were cops, I suddenly gained my composure, and faked a story. "My name is Lien, and I am stationed in Dong Ba Thin, in the vicinity of the Cam Ranh Bay area. My unit is working on a salt farm, and my commander is Le van Nghien (my father's name). It is Sunday, today. I came to pay Mr. Man a visit. Mr. Man and I grew up in the same village in the Northern part of the country."

Thank God, they seemed to buy my story, but the other one threw me a last but critical command. "Show me your ID!"

I told them that it was a day off, being a Sunday, and I had taken off from my unit without any personal papers with me, and if they wanted, they could call my unit for verification. That did it! For now they turned to Mr. Man to ask him a lot more questions.

"Why haven't you been fishing the last few months?" the officers questioned.

"I haven't been feeling well and have to go into town for medical help," Mr. Man answered.

They immediately ordered Man to follow them to the police station.

As they got out of the house, I sneaked back into the kitchen, where Man's wife was sitting. I pulled out from my pocket the two bars of twenty-four-karat gold and immediately gave them to her and asked her to bury them into the ashes at her cooking stove at once. These bars of gold were given to Mr. Man so that he could give them to his parents, who decided not to come along. If they ever caught me with gold in my possession, one could not have imagined what kind of trouble I could get myself into. Just as soon as I returned to my seat in the living room, one of the cops came back into the front door and signaled that I must come with them to their headquarters.

It was a sunny and hot day; the bare dirt road heading to the police station seemed never to end. Every now and then, a whirlwind stirred colored dust into the air as if to sadden our situation and dampen my hope of escaping. What would be waiting for me at the end of the road? What would happen if they unmasked me as a fake soldier or a fake cop? *At the police headquarters, there must be more seasoned and skillful cops who could beat me at their own game,* I thought. We were walking single file, one cop in front and the other in the back. A few passersby gave curious looks. From their perspective, it may have appeared that the three cops were escorting one suspect, Mr. Man, and my uniform was camouflaging my suspect status. I was trying to remember exactly what I had told them so that I could stick to this story when I arrived at the police station, where I expected that the interrogation would be very intense. I was praying that I could keep my composure and get through this without any flaws. I was quite surprised at myself for being so calm when unexpectedly confronted with the two cops a while ago at Mr. Man's house. It must have come from a spirit above because I could never have been able to do it by myself.

I now was worried about my wife, who had been undergoing a lot of hardship every time I was caught attempting to escape. It was not easy for her to take care of our two sons, Lam and Tuan, who were only in kindergarten, as well as of her parents and her siblings. I had promised myself not to engage in any activities that would put me in a situation in which the government could send me back to prison and the labor camps. Unfortunately, just as soon as I was released from my imprisonment, seeing that the reality of life outside of the prison was just another prison on a larger scale, I broke that promise again! I could see no future for my children, for they would never be allowed to go to school because of my past. Because of my service with the former government, I was now considered an outcast, or enemy of the people, and therefore the rest of my family and I were driven out of our habitat. The jungle was where we would be dropped off to start our new life.

I had completely lost trust in this new regime, whose tactics in getting us out of our house were very inhumane. In one way you were being threatened to hand over your house, your property to the government for the very reason that you had served the former government; you were the enemy of the people, as you were told, and therefore you did not deserve to stay in the house, in the property you had owned years before the new government came to power. However, on the other hand, to prevent them from international scrutiny, which might condemn their policy of oppressing and mistreating their citizens, they asked us to sign a quit claim form, or, to be exact, a letter of offering stating that "we hereby voluntarily offer the government our house, our property, and by the grace of our government, we are, in turn, given a place to live and to work in the new economy zone." How can you trust a government that robs you and makes you sign an agreement that you are offering to them what they have stolen from you?

"Go faster," ordered the cop behind me, as if he wanted me to hurry to be confronted by his boss, or else he was anxious to see me accused and thrown in the local cell. Either way, I wondered if I'd ever know his thoughts. The faces of these cops and the cops I had seen on the street and everywhere else were always stoic and cold. One could never tell if there were any thoughts behind those emotionless faces that had a touch of love or of caring. If they did, they'd never allow it to show. It always made you feel nervous.

"Sit down," commanded the young officer at this local police station as I was escorted into his office. At least I did not feel threaten by this young fellow. Maybe he was more educated, or perhaps he was more sophisticated in his character and his profession. Or maybe the uniform on me had some influence in the way he looked at me. Either way, he was quite handsome in his uniform, a light orange-colored khaki pants and a shirt with a high collar. The two red and gold straps on both of his shoulders showed off his authority: I am a police officer!

"What are you doing here in this village?" he asked. But it was not in an interrogative tone of voice; instead, it was more like a casual inquiry from a friend or an acquaintance. I told him that I had come to pay my friend a visit and that I was stationed in the Cam Ranh Bay area and so on and so forth. I almost repeated what I had told the other two cops earlier. Right then he looked at me and said that since I did not have any identification, I should not stay in the village overnight and I must remember to carry my ID on my next visit to stay out of trouble. That was it! Short and sweet and simple, you might say. All along, I was worried how to deal with this supposedly sophisticated cop, and I also imagined that the interrogation could be gruelingly unpleasant. But obviously he had treated me like his comrade in arms. How could I explain this whole thing, a sort of a miracle? I attributed it to some invisible hands, to the spirit that must have worked in the situation and freed me from the Communist police officer. I thanked him, and I went home with Man.

Once outside the police station, I felt as if I had wings lifting me up from a load of a thousand tons. I breathed with relief. I could not have imagined what would have happened if they had decided to keep me in there for further investigation. The prison and the labor camp would be waiting for me, and what would have happened next I certainly would not want to know.

It was still warm on this sunny day. Man and I really enjoyed our walking home but kept quiet most of the time, knowing that it was a very close call for all of us. He would have probably blamed me for unexpectedly showing up at his house and getting him in trouble. Now, however, he realized for the first time that he and his family had been watched twenty-four hours a day for months. I asked Man to prepare lunch at his house and said that we needed to discuss our plan to escape as soon as it got dark. A quick lunch was served with rice and some dried fish, but it was all so tasty. For one thing, we were hungry, and another, we survived an almost fiasco. We quickly got into the plans of action for the night in which he would have to pretend or act as if he were going on a fishing trip in the evening with his selected crew to escape on his boat. His wife and his children would then have to come with me on the bus to join my wife and my children and other people in the Cam Ranh Bay area.

From his village, Long Huong, where his boat would start heading to Cam Ranh water, he would have to bring his fishing boat to the outside of the mouth of the bay and anchor at the point of rendezvous and stay put, waiting for us to come.

Our best estimate time to meet him at the mouth of Cam Ranh Bay was about one o'clock in the morning. He understood the plan well, and he knew that if he made any mistakes, his family, my family, and families of others would be on the line.

When I arrived back in the Cam Ranh area together with the rest of Man's family, my wife and everyone was so happy to see me because they had been told about our arrest in the village earlier in the day. When the messenger girl, my little guide, returned to the bay area, she gave them the news after she had witnessed the two cops escort both of us to the police station. It was such devastating news to her and the rest of the group because without me, without Mr. Man, there would be no boat, and all plans of escape would be futile. Worst of all, my wife would see the jail cells awaiting me.

Immediately our group members were contacted and taken to hide inside the houses of the fishermen who would, for a price of two hundred thousand piasters (dong) per head, take one or two persons onto their fishing boats, cover them with the nets, and row them off the shore as if the boat were on a fishing trip. The villagers in this particular area had been doing this for quite some time, mostly for money, and they had done it quite well. They knew the risks of doing this, for if they got caught, it meant prison. They were always careful and tight-lipped and very selective about their "customers," as they worked on referral basis only.

At three o'clock in the morning, the news came in through a liaison person that Mr. Man and his crew had not come. His boat was nowhere to be seen, and no one knew what had happened to it. What went through my mind were a number of scenarios, one of which was that he had probably been caught as he was taking off from his village. But it wouldn't have happened; it could not be true, as he had had all legitimate reasons to take off with his boat to go on his fishing trip. No one could stop him from going except he himself. He may have chickened out and decided not to go at all. But this also had no grounds because his wife and his kids were with us through the evening, and they were still in this village. Another scenario could be that maybe his boat had mechanical problems and had not been able to make it there on time. What else could have happened? Question after question, and I had no answers.

I and other friends in our leadership group had decided to let everyone know that they needed to go home before dawn and to go on with their business as usual until we got ahold of Man and his boat. They also needed to be very careful when leaving their hideouts. They were instructed not to carry anything—no luggage or any personal belongings. Any bags would certainly invite scrutiny from the cops and the passersby. One person getting caught would jeopardize the safety of the whole group. It was a big sacrifice that everyone had to think of for the safety of everyone else.

At noon the news came in from the liaison person that the boat and the crew had been located and were now anchored, waiting for us at the mouth of the Cam Ranh Bay. The news certainly brought joy and energy to our group, and our plan was immediately put back into motion. Everyone was going to be contacted and ready for the second night of adventure, and the hideouts would be the same. All procedures of the previous night would be carefully repeated.

Later on during the day, we learned that the reason for the boat not showing up the night before was that it ran out of fuel, and as result, it drifted to an island where a small unit of coastal guards was staying. Man was able to get some fuel from the soldiers in trade for his gold ring, just enough to get him to the mouth of Cam Ranh Bay. All of us in the leadership group were very unhappy with him over this incident, which truly endangered our lives and delayed our trip. Many months prior to our departure, Man had been given money, time after time, to buy fuel and provisions for our trip, and he was supposed to do this quietly, secretly, on his own. He was also supposed to hide them in the bushes along the shoreline little by little every time he went fishing. As it now turned out, he had not done any of those things and had probably spent all the money lavishly to the extent that it caused attention from the local cops, and that was the very reason that he had been under watch twenty-four hours a day.

Man should be punished for his selfish behavior, but we had to save our energy and our wisdom for getting everyone to the boat. There would be lots of challenges ahead of us; any flaw to the execution of our plan meant prison or death. We could not afford either of those outcomes.

It was late in the evening; we had been going without incident for almost a day. We wondered how many more days ahead before we could reach the shoreline of the Philippines. This boat had been doing a very good job so far. It had left many miles behind its wake since early that morning. The load on this fishing craft was enormous, for I was able to reach down to touch the water with my hands. I did not want to think about the situation where we would encounter bad weather. It would be very scary, for I doubted that it would stand a chance.

This open sea, this water, this vastness of the sky, this feeling of freedom I had been longing for for many years had now come to a reality. This certainly was the fruit of many hours, many days of labor, and many nights of planning. We had carried out each little step—from contacting a friend, talking to acquaintances to get them involved (making sure that none of them was an undercover agent), to scouting, following the trails through the woods that led to the beaches to familiarize ourselves with the landscape and environment. This often was done at night to avoid cops and patrols from the government soldiers. My friend and companion, Ngoc Nguyen, and I had spent many hours, many nights in which we crossed the river, braved the woods, and walked over numerous dunes of sands to get to the cliffs looking over the sea. We would sit there soaking in everything the sea had to offer from the breezes to the sounds of the crashing waves. At the same time, we talked about our plans of escape, our dreams of new life beyond the sea. Twinkling lights from a thousand fishing boats out in the vast water only intensified our desire to escape.

Each step of the process involved some sort of risks. The riskiest thing was to have an undercover cop on your boat at the final hour of the departure. There had been many incidents in which the boat people who, at the time of their taking off from the shoreline, found themselves arrested at gunpoint by non-uniformed cops who had been working along with them from the beginning of their plans of escape. The result was that they ended up in prison and then the labor camp. Making contacts with the right people was always a difficult and careful process. The society had somehow become one that created doubt and fear of one person to another. Children at school were taught to spy on their parents and were to report to their teachers any activities at home that they deemed to be abnormal, be it a visit from a friend, a relative, or just an absence of a parent from home. An old friend and acquaintance from yesterday could become someone who could turn you in for what you said and did.

Yes, I now could push all of this behind, like this boat, longing for the new water, breathing the fresh air, and I was very grateful for that. It was late in the evening, and the day was almost over. The crew was getting ready for the night shift. The boat captain, Mr. Ngoi, had decided to take a night break to rejuvenate himself, so he handed the control over to his friend, an old friend and neighbor fisherman. They both had had many hours of sea life, but of course, never in the high sea, in the deep sea. Nevertheless, he was in the cabin with his wife and children, and their showing of joy brought assurance and happiness to everyone in the boat.

My mind was wandering back to the old days when I had my first thoughts of escaping to foreign lands by boat, crossing the sea. The thoughts had turned into plans, and I then actually stepped on the boat and became a pioneer of the boat people in the central coastal region of Vietnam, who began a daring trip heading to the Philippines. It all started at the fall of the Saigon government, which had quickly fallen into the hand of the Communists in 1975. All of us men who had served the former government were taken to prison, the so-called "re-education" camps, with a promise that all would be sent home in a very short period of time, one week. As if to reinforce the prospect of going home within that time frame, we were asked to bring with us provisions enough for seven days. But one week turned into one month, and months turned into a year, and year after year, and many of us never had a chance to see our families, our loved ones again.

Upon entering the camp, or to be exact, the prison, one would be given a form to fill out. It was sort of a personal profile that included a personal history from the time of birth, places of schooling, places of work, and duration of service to the military or to different branches of government. It was not an easy task. One would always be reminded by the guards, "The more you tell us about yourself, about what you have done, the sooner you will be going home to your family, and remember that you are the people's enemy; and because of the grace of the party, the grace of this government, you have a chance to be here to redeem yourselves."

Everyone knew it was a trap, but to avoid it was not easy. Each night the Communists would tell every one of us at the meeting that they had everyone's records at the central government database and that they knew everyone's position and performance in the former regime; therefore it was up to each one of us to make that honest confession about our past because "the more you tell, the sooner . . . ." There had been many who had fallen to this trap and had never had a chance to return to see their families, as they were quietly transferred to remote prison camps in the jungles of North Vietnam.

As my stay entered into the second week, I noticed that there were three non-Vietnamese prisoners among us in this camp. They were Filipinos who happened to be in the very wrong place at the very wrong time and were picked up by the local guards to be put in this facility as a precautionary measure against any foreigners at the end of the war. They were kind of isolated because they did not know the language and worst of all, did not know what the Communists would do to them. As I approached them at lunchtime and asked them to follow the line of people who were heading to the kitchen to get food for their lunch, they were extremely happy that I could communicate with them in English. They told me the reason for them to come to the Cam Ranh area was to look for their wives, who were thought to be in the area at that time. Unfortunately, they were arrested and taken into prison by the Communists, who suspected that they were some sort of sleeping agents working for the US government.

Unlike many of us who had been made to fill out all kinds of papers just as soon as we arrived at the camp, these folks had not been interviewed, nor had they been asked to fill out any forms or any questionnaire. Of course, there were no forms to be used, and none of which were in English available to the unexpected guests. These poor fellows were worried and felt hopeless due to the fact that no one would understand what they were up to, and to make the matter worse, the language barrier had prohibited them from telling their side of the story.

As the days went by, I was busy at my new assignment as a clerk for the internal security group, which would make sure everything inside the camp was in order from food services to scheduling the labor teams working outside of the camp. I had not had much time to think and to talk to our new friends, and besides, I really did not want the guards to know that I could speak foreign languages, especially English, for it is the language of America, the language of the enemy, the language of imperialism.

At the end of the day, however, I was summoned to see the officer in charge of the camp, a captain from the North Vietnamese Army. What I was afraid of now became reality. I made contact with the foreigner; I spoke English to the foreigner right inside the camp. My charges, my penalty could be doubled or even tripled. I thought about it with a little nervousness.

"You speak English?" the commander asked me with an amicable voice as soon as I was ushered into his office, which was lit up with an oil lamp that barely helped me to judge his age and his appearance.

"Yes, sir," I answered, and I told him how long I had been speaking English, as he demanded to know. He did not waste much time as he told me that he believed that these Filipinos were members of CIA and that they were here in the Cam Ranh area for their mission against the socialistic government of Vietnam. My assignment from him was to watch them, to follow them, and then to report back to him, and that was all I had to do. He dismissed me after my promise to take on my new duty, my new mission.

Outside of his office, it was all so quiet except the faint cricket cries outside the barbed-wire fence, and the air stilled with a fragrance of the blossoms of a dwarf papaya tree. The moon was bright and high above, and I was walking back to my little corner where I had my hammock. Suddenly, I felt very tired and scared of what I was asked to do. For all my life, I had never done anything of this nature, and this was spying for the Communists. But here I was just a prisoner, a captive at their mercy. I might go home to my family sooner, perhaps, if I did what I was told, or the consequences could be unimaginable; my choice was so very limited. Or did I have choice? It must have been very late at night, for it was also very quiet. The people next to me were sound asleep. I just hoped that no one would know what my new assignment was. To be an informant, a spy, or the best described term *antenna,* used in the prison, for the Communists would certainly earn me a spot on the traitors' list that would stay with me for the rest of my life, and I could not afford to have it. My heart felt so heavy as my body sank down on the hammock; the mosquitoes outside the net seemed to understand my dilemma with their singing.

The following days I was not given any laborious duties such as going into the jungle to fetch logs or going to the field for farming tasks. Instead, I was assigned to a more sophisticated one; that was, to watch our new Filipino friends to make sure that they were what they were thought to be: the CIA in disguise, working against the new revolutionary government. With this new line of duty, I enjoyed the fact that I could enhance my language skills by interacting with my new friends using English and learning their language as well. What was so obvious to everyone in the prison camp was that I did not have to do any labor work like many other prisoners. This set me apart from the crowd and drew both favorable and unfavorable reactions from them. Jealousy was to become most noticeable from my fellow camp prisoners. But I did appreciate the fact that I did not have to battle the heat and the sun in the field, bringing back the logs for firewood.

I was able to hang around with Benjamin, the tallest of the three, and the other two, who were named Marcelino and Gomez, all days and most of the evenings. We shared with one another the stories of our childhood up to the adulthood, from families to the societies and so on. We shared our religious faith and our hopes for the future if we could ever get out from this prison alive. For now, we had had no clue if and when we would be released to go home to our families. We had much laughter together as we shared our many stories and innumerable jokes to make our time in this prison memorable. We also found out that some of vocabulary of Tagalog, the main language of the Philippines, was very much similar to that of Rhade, the Montagnard tribal people in Ban Me Thuot, the central highland of Vietnam. I used to tease them that their ancestors must have come from Vietnam many, many hundred years ago when they decided that they needed to go out to explore their new world across the sea and found the Philippines.

One evening not too long after my assignment, I told them about what the director of the camp had thought about them and that I had not believed they were in any way undercover for the US intelligence. I also told them that they should watch their behavior, their language, and not say what should not be said. After hearing this, they became quiet for some moments in the darkness of the evening. Their minds were probably wandering into the unknown, the uncertainty, for now they were being suspected as hands for the CIA. I shared with them my thoughts and that they should not be worried, for I would always be watching out for them and I would be telling the management of the camp that they were just some simple, normal, working Filipinos who got caught at the tail end of the war and who did not have enough time to get out of the country. Ben and other guys were very appreciative of the fact that I was on their side and that I was doing my very best to win their release from this prison camp.

Weeks had gone by in the camp with lots of emotion and anxiety among the prisoners. Some new ones were rifle-escorted into the camp, and some were loaded into canvas-covered vehicles and then taken away in the evening, God only knows where. Every day seemed to have newcomers, and every day there were some to be hauled away. No one knew when it would be his turn to be taken away, and it seemed that it happened almost always in the evening before dark. It was as if darkness was associated with loneliness and was frightening to the weak, the meek, the losers, and the prisoners. One evening, it was dark and quiet; Ben whispered to me that he had something to share with me.

"Do not be so discouraged, brother! If you really want to get out of Vietnam, you can do so, and I will show you ways and how because I'm a sea merchant who has crossed the seas and oceans many times."

Ben later shared his experiences and showed me when it was the best time to do it and how to sail. And it was because of Ben that my hope of going abroad to America always stayed alive amid all obstacles and difficulties.

The day I was told to relay the decision from the Communist camp management that they were to be released to go home to their families was just a pure joy and a happy day for my friends and for me too. I was pleased at the notion that I had somehow accomplished my inner mission, fulfilled my promise, which was to protect them, and with their freedom to go home today, it was my unpronounced success as well.

With a handshake and a hug to each of them, I wished them a safe trip home to Manila and told them that I was going to miss them very much and we would meet someday in the Philippines. Ben handed me a souvenir as he was leaving, his orange-colored pants, his favorite that he had worn during his stay. I accepted his gift with deep appreciation.

Upon my release from the camp, I registered to become a fisherman, as many elders who had quite a lot experiences with the Communists had advised me. I had learned from them that out in the sea, no one could have control over your catch; therefore one can have one's fill without worrying about being watched or reported by secret agents. This could be anyone with whom you are dealing on a daily basis; it could be your neighbor, your friend, or even your own children, who are being taught at school that they should watch their parents and report to their school for all activities and behavior. It was sad but true.

My very first fishing craft was purchased with a little money left from our savings. It was made out of tin sheet metal sixteen-feet-by-six-feet, sort of like a canoe but with a small diesel motor. It became my pal; I worked with it and at it every single day. I realized that this size boat would never carry my family and me across the island, the bay, let alone the sea. My imagination could only go wilder as time passed by. I needed a bigger boat and a more powerful engine to be able to get the job done. But, first things first, I had to be able to legally upgrade the size of this baby of mine. A newly released prisoner like me lost all rights and privileges under the eyes of current regime, and to have it grant me an approval to enlarge the boat was just a part of my wildest dream. But I comforted myself with a thought that anything big needs time as well as patience and good planning on how to achieve it, and then comes action.

I immediately put my plan into motion. Every day on my fishing trips I learned to use my nets, and then I learned to build and to use bamboo cage-traps, which was initially a challenge. But as time went on, it became an enjoyable hobby. It was an art of making the bamboo traps and did not require lots of work, as it did with the nets. Staying up late, waiting for the right time, and learning to lower nets into the water was something I had to get myself used to.

And by doing so very diligently, I escaped the watchful eyes of the local cops and doubtful neighbors, and indeed, I earned the friendship and trust from the village chief, whom I would visit almost weekly at the end of the day just when it got dark to be sure the observations of the neighbors and the passersby was minimal. I would save some nice fish or crab from my catch to give him as gifts, and he and his family seemed to enjoy my visits and happily accepted the offerings.

One day, long after I was well into my fishing career, I felt that the time had come for me to act, as our friendship had matured and a higher level of trust had been reached, even though one of us was an appointed government official and the other a newly released prisoner. One night I came over to his house with an application requesting authorization to enlarge my fishing boat. I told him that I would like to have a bigger boat so that I could do a better job of fishing, as I would be able to go out farther into the sea where it was deeper and therefore, get a better catch. Without hesitation, he went inside his room to get his pen and then slowly sat down at his dusty desk cluttered with numerous things. He tried to glance through my application under the oil lamp, then scribbled a few words of recommendation for approval and handed the application to me with advice that I should stay out of trouble. It was as if he had already read my mind, my plans. I thanked him for his help and dashed out of his house into the darkness, immersing myself in the quiet of the night. I could hear my feet pounding on the street. I wanted to scream out loud to let out my excitement and my joy as I was running straight home. I began to know and to visualize that my plan of getting a bigger boat for my escape was materializing.

The next morning as I walked out of the office of the security chief of the village where I obtained the final stamp of approval for my project, I felt so happy that the birds outside on the trees seemed to understand my feeling and to congratulate me with melodies of their songs. The sky seemed to be clearer and wide open, as if it were giving me an air of freedom. I was so lifted in this spirit that I felt I could fly away. I was now mentally painting a picture of a few others and myself on my future boat, cruising in and out of the mouth of Cam Ranh Bay and ultimately in the South China Sea. What a thrill it would be!

Moving my boat to a location where it was going to get expanded was not as easy a job as I had hoped. First, I had to take the boat passing under the bridge, where the checkpoint was set up to control all movement on the river. I was thinking that I had my paperwork giving me permission; therefore I should not have had any problem. What I did not know was that I was supposed to somehow get permission for passing through the bridge, sort of a day pass, before any attempt to bring the boat across that checkpoint on the water at the bridge began. As a result of my assumption, coupled with my ignorance, what happened next was a scary, ugly scene.

As I was approaching the bridge, a couple of guards with rifles standing on the side of the bridge screamed from top of their lungs and a rain of bullets came down, splashing water onto my boat. I did not know if they really wanted to aim at me and missed, or if it was just the way they stopped people. Whatever their tactic was, it worked well, for I was scared to death and pulled my boat over to the shore at their command. I was let go after one of the soldiers conducted a brief search of my boat, which contained barely anything except a few pieces of personal belongings and my letter of authorization, which allowed me to move my boat to its destination for reconstruction. What an eventful evening! And what happened if those bullets rained down on my boat and one or two of them landed on me? One does not need to guess.

At Xuan Ninh Village, just as soon as my boat got pulled off the water, the crew immediately dismantled it to pieces, which then all got piled up at a corner of the beach to become firewood and junk. The project for the bigger boat was started right away. The size of it was going to become three times the size of the former one, but not so big that it would cause any suspicion from the local authorities. A mechanic friend would help provide a transmission from a discarded jeep, which would be hooked up and run by a ten-horsepower diesel engine. The friend who would supervise the installation explained that the transmission would be used and installed in a reverse position, which would generate a more powerful drive for the larger-sized prop. I was there at the site just about every day and sometimes at night to watch the handcrafted piece of artwork being formed from nothing more than sheets of one-inch planks of wood into the shape of the boat. Heating them over the fire did the curving of some pieces, and the caulking of the seams to prevent leaks was done using melted sap of trees. These were very primitive but very effective ways of building boats from these folks in this village.

Every now and then, I would come to this boat-building site to get inspired by the sounds of sawing, of chisels pounding on the wood, and mostly from the incense-like smell of the tree sap being melted over the fire, all of which would surely stretch my imagination far into the sea. These workers and their foreman worked so hard for the money they received. What amazed me was that they created this without a single sheet of blueprints. All was in their head; nothing was written, nothing was drawn. They kept making boat after boat, the one with motor or the one without, the sailboat, in different sizes. There were times sailboats were being considered in our plans. They certainly did not need fuel, and there were no mechanical failures to worry about. There was no risk of being caught stocking up fuel supplies, but the dark side of it was it would not move on the windless days. This picture was not very enticing and sometimes quite a scary one.

The final day of its completion was approaching. The air was a lot cooler, and the wind was faintly shifting its direction from north to south, signaling summer was coming to its final days. The rumor was traveling fast in the village that my boat was about to get launched for a test run, and they said I was about ready to escape to America. These kinds of rumors certainly did not help me one bit; in fact, they may have done some damage to my plans.

Finally she was in the water for the first time. It was a beautiful, sunny day in the cloudless blue sky, and the water was pristine clear. We took her out all the way to the mouth of the bay. She performed and behaved quite well on the water, as expected. She glided on the water very fast, even though I did not know how fast in terms of miles or knots. But it was fast enough to heighten my joy and my excitement. Just about every day, I would take her out to get to know her and make sure that I was building up my routine on my runs, sometimes with my kids and other times with friends on the boat during afternoon hours, as I hoped that some day I would take off during the daylight, which would be a surprise to everyone, including the local cops. For so long, all escapes had taken place at nighttime, when the patrols were always on the watch.

It was in the afternoon hours in mid-July, and the sun was bright. The breeze was gentle enough to move the palm branches at the beach. Some kids in the village were enjoying swimming in the water where I anchored my boat. The fuel was in the tank, and a few extra cans were tucked away in the engine compartment. Food was mostly in dry form such as roasted rice or dehydrated potatoes and cassava. Drinking water was fresh in a few containers stored under the deck. Everything seemed to be in the mood for a takeoff.

My wife and my two sons and my younger brother-in-law had been in the boat since the early morning hours. My two sons were too young to be informed about the trip that would take them to the faraway land. I could read and feel the anxiety in my wife's face. She was about to leave her parents and her brothers and sisters for a journey that would never give her a chance to see them again. But for the sake of our children's future, she and I had to take on this path, and it was not an easy one. The ideas and excitement, if any, of embarking into the unknown would bear no comparison to the agony and sadness of leaving her birthplace, her relatives and friends, and her world of childhood.

As minutes ticked by while I was waiting for other friends and companions to show up for the trip, I happened to notice that there were a few young people seated or roaming in the vicinity of my boat, and the number seemed to increase as time went by. Finally it dawned on me that these unfamiliar faces were here because they heard about our trip and they wanted to come on board. But also, who knew if any among them was an undercover agent who would wait for me to make a move then put handcuffs on me, I wondered! No one could tell! And I was beginning to get nervous to see my friends. As my companions started to emerge from the crowd, which really grew by the minute, I realized that it would be almost impossible to take off without some sort of trouble. First, the bystanders, or the unwanted passengers, would just climb onto the boat, and there was nothing anyone or I could do about it. They would just be screaming out loud if I tried to stop them from coming to the boat. Second, if I let everyone on, the boat would sink right there before it even had any chance to move.

There was nothing I could do to improve the situation. The chosen and unwanted ones had the very same desire, a very strong one to leave and to get on my boat regardless of the outcome. I then had to make a very quick decision that was to abort my plan. I told my group of people to return to their homes and that my wife would take my boys out of the boat so that the crowd would let me move my boat out into the deeper water. And as my family members took off from the boat and I started the engine to pull the boat away, the people on the beach began to disappear into the village behind the lines of coconut palm tress. I had a very strong feeling that trouble was about to happen to me, for there would be someone from that very crowd who was an informant, an undercover agent who had seen what was going on in the afternoon, would file a report, and then the cops, with rifles and handcuffs, would come.

PRISON AND RE-EDUCATION

When my boat was about three-quarters of a mile off the shoreline, heading to the inlet to stay overnight, from the corner of my eyes, I saw the water splash from the side of the boat—one, two, three, and a lot more; then I heard the gunshots. Coming toward me was a gunboat with policemen in orange-colored uniforms, and their guns were aimed at me. They used their hand-held loudspeaker to order me to stop the boat and to surrender to them with my arms up to the sky. Everything happened so fast from the moment of seeing the water splash along the side of my boat, thinking it was from fish playing, to the dire realization that those splashes were from bullets, that I barely had time to react. The sound of the gunshots and the order to surrender all came like lightning and thunder. Two of the cops jumped onto my boat. One had his rifle pointed at me, and the other started searching in the cabin of the boat, where he found Sy, my young brother-in-law, who, after a couple of slaps on his face, confessed to the cops that I was engaging in an attempt to escape. Besides his confession, there was no other evidence supporting my plan of escape. Nevertheless, both of us were then immediately taken into the local jail for preliminary investigation and interrogation. That very night, hungry, cold, and exhausted, I tasted the salty taste of my own blood when a cop, the interrogator, surprised me with his right-hand punch on my face, drawing blood from the left corner of my mouth when I refused to tell him about my escape plans involving other people.

The next morning we were dropped off and escorted to the road heading to the district jail. As we were walking toward the gate of the jail, I noticed my wife was standing at the side of the road waiting for me. She must have been devastated at the news that we both were caught and taken to the district prison. She must have not had any sleep, for she was very tired and sad. She then asked for permission from the escort guards to hand me some clothes and some personal items, all of which would be checked at the entrance. We could not say much, except that I told her how sorry I was for this happening and that she should bring our boys to let them stay with our friend Ms. Phung in Saigon so that she could be free to do some work at the market to bring food home for the whole family. She bade me farewell in tears and walked away to the main road to catch her ride home, and I continued my walk to the jail cell dejectedly.

This would be my third time in the Communist prison in less than two years, and, as always, she had to absorb the whole responsibility of taking care of the large family—her parents, her brothers and sisters, our children, and now, me, a prisoner who would provide no income to the family. Instead, I had now become a burden. I felt guilt and disappointment in me as I was taken into the cell where a number of male prisoners were getting ready for their daily labor work in the field outside the compound. I was more worried about my wife and my children than I was scared of anything that might be coming to me. I had tasted the physical abuses and mental torture from my previous confinements, and whatever more of it came my way, I would certainly try to handle it the best I could without any regret or complaint.

Later on during the day, I was given paper and pen to start writing my own statement of what was going on yesterday, what my intentions were, what steps I had planned, and so on. It was some sort of confession admitting the fact that I was engaging in organizing a trip crossing the sea to a foreign country, and that I must tell the authorities the names of those who participated in this trip physically and financially. I had been in and out of their prison and their system long enough to understand their ways of collecting information. Any information given that related to anyone behind the scenes of my plan meant imprisonment for them. I would never ever fall into any of those tactics of extracting information and details.

I had in the past and would always stick to my original statement without modification, regardless of any form of threats. This had helped me thus far in dealing with the Communist system. Those behind the scene and I had had personal agreement and promised that in case of one being caught, he and he alone would bear the consequences. No one else's names would be mentioned or given, as if that person had never existed in life. This would give whoever was out there, behind the scenes, a chance to do whatever it took to win the release for the one who got caught, and I knew in my heart this was happening right now outside this fenced-in barbed-wire prison. This would begin with my wife, who would be contacting a high-ranking official, Mr. Hoang, whom I came to know through my second imprisonment when my very first attempt of escape became a fiasco. This contact person had become a secret pal to our family and also had helped many people in the community, as well as in the region. Hoang always kept himself very low profile in our relationship. Most of my rendezvous with him happened in the dark and almost always at his residence, where I sometimes joined his wife and his children for dinner. He earned my trust as a person who could do more help and no harm. Throughout months of knowing him, he never asked me to do any work for him such as becoming an informant, nor was I ever asked to provide information that a cop would be looking for. Instead, I had a chance to test him, to peek into his mind and his heart to see whether or not he was genuinely a friend or a highly sophisticated cop who had had six years of training in the Soviet police academy and who would one day turn me in or ask me to turn someone in.

One night I pulled up all my courage to ask him a question.

This took place at my house when he was coming home from his meeting in Nha Trang. I hypothetically created a scenario in which I was asked by a group of people, most of whom were Chinese, who would pay me a hefty fee, a bar of gold for each person, if I were to transport them from the inland to the other side of the river with my boat so that they could walk across the island to catch their boat at the shoreline. The fees would be paid up front, and the delivery would be done right after dark, which would allow them enough time to catch their boat ride and also to minimize the risk of being spotted during the move. My question to him was done in such a way as if I were seeking advice to see if it would be wise to engage in such activity. I thought I knew him well enough. Sharing meals with him, I truly believed that he was genuinely a good friend—no more, no less. There have been times I have thought he was a God-sent angel who came to my life and to the lives of others to help and to ease our pain. His answer, or his advice in this case, was that I should go ahead making my move and then he would come with his troops to net his rewards, or he would advise me against doing it. I presented this question to him with all seriousness of the matter in my voice, waiting for the same gravity in his reply. An answer of yes or no would determine my fate, my relationship or my friendship with him.

He then specifically told me that I should not be unwise as to participate in such activity, for if at any time during their journey they were caught, I'd be in trouble for being their accomplice. I should be patient so that someday he would help me fulfill my dream, a dream of going far very far away from this troubled land to which I was born and love with all my heart.

I was taken into a metal container called a conex box, a medical supply container left behind by the US military. I was told not to make any noise or to talk to anyone and that I would be allowed to come out from this box once a day, only in the morning, for thirty minutes. I was ushered inside, and after the metal door was slammed shut and the cold sound of a padlock clicked on the door as if it were signaling the end of my dream for freedom, I was immersed in almost complete darkness in the space of less than one hundred cubic feet. There were tiny trails of light coming in from a few little bullet holes on the walls of the metal box. The heat from the afternoon sun, the smell of rusted metal combined with the smell of something decaying in this box gave me a creepy feeling.

I was once told a story that if you let a mouse into a room where another mouse was killed, this mouse would immediately detect something unfriendly in the air and would find his way out right away. I tried to get myself familiarized with the space and the light and darkness of the room, wondering who and what had been here and what had happened to them. I began to sweat, maybe because of the temperature inside the box or because of the lack of air; or was it because of something inside me, or the combination of all? Is this what claustrophobia is all about? Whatever the cause was, I would never know.

Later on in the evening, there was the sound of the door being unlocked, and the guard and a kitchen helper appeared at the door to pass in a bowl of rice with a few grains of salt and quietly left after the door was locked shut. I was so very tired, and it was hard to eat, even though I had not eaten for the last twenty-four hours. I had lost my appetite and looked at the rice, wondering about the relationship between the portion of food and amount of time allowed to be outside for discharge. It was relatively equivalent! Less to eat, less the need to toilet—it was all in the plan. I began to wonder how or if I knew how to cope with tomorrow's heat and other unknowns and surprises. I was so exhausted by all the events that had happened that I fell asleep on the floor. I was awakened to the sound of a gong, a wake-up call for all prisoners, and then, as scheduled, everyone was allowed a maximum of thirty minutes for wash-ups and hygiene activities. When I was let out of the box and led to the washroom, it dawned on me that I had held off all the needs of going to the restroom for such a long time, perhaps almost twelve hours, and now I really needed it.

At the restroom, there was one toilet hole in a space of about fifty or sixty square feet. There were no doors, and the floor was wet, combining with a heavy bathroom smell. There were a few other guys who were naked, bathing by scooping the water from a metal drum that was rusted from the outside and was still held together because it was originally an asphalt container. The reddish-brown color of water inside the fifty-five-gallon drum, which was fed with a one-inch clear plastic hose from a water pond nearby, gave me a feeling that the water was not safe for drinking. The rusted metal flakes that moved at each scoop of water were the ones that gave this unhealthy, unclean-looking color too. I shielded my shamelessness and swallowed my pride, rushing next to the man who was squatting on the toilet hole. He moved a little to accommodate me without saying a word, perhaps because he felt the very same pain that we were all having in this situation. Perhaps he understood that we were in the same boat and that we needed to show some kindness and caring to each other.

I was escorted back to the box after my allotted time was up, during which I was able to do a quick bath by scooping a couple buckets of water from a water drum nearby and letting it run from my head down. Oh heavens, I felt quite refreshed after a few days without a bath. I was also able to fill a plastic bottle with water from the container for drinking, and later on in the day, when it got really hot inside the metal box, I used it to every now and then pour a little on my head to cool myself off from the rising temperature in this seemingly giant oven. During the day, I would be escorted to the office for questioning, filling out forms, and making a confession statement. Every day I would be asked to do the same thing, and at the end of each session, I was reminded that the more truthful my confession, the sooner I was to go home. This seemed to be a sugarcoated pill used by the Communists since their early existence.

My life in this box was fortunately cut short. In just one week, thanks to Mr. Hoang's intervention behind the scene, I was sent to serve my time at the labor camp, Khanh Son, in the jungle about fifty miles away from the city. I found myself in an open truck that hauled a few of us prisoners and an armed guard in the morning hour, heading west of the Cam Ranh Bay toward the mountains and jungles. Despite what lay ahead, we were in pretty good spirits. At this moment, we enjoyed the fresh air and knew that we were a step closer to going home. We began our journey of labor just as soon as we were about halfway to the labor camp. The truck stopped at the side of a creek, and the guard signaled us to get off the vehicle. One by one we would walk on a "monkey bridge," which was a tree that somehow fell across the water.

As we walked all the way to the labor camp, we noticed the guard wasn't as bad as those at the prison. He seemed to have a kindhearted spirit about him, as he encouraged singing and talking among us. Of course, the songs allowed in public in those days were about Uncle Ho Chi Minh and his party and the warriors and the wars that were gallantly won by the people. It seemed that songs and political speeches were daily and nightly activities at every corner of the country. It was done to the extent that it became so very boring, so perfunctory and meaningless.

Upon arrival at the so-called Khanh Son labor camp, I was assigned to a bamboo barrack where there were some other men who were having a noon break before they began their afternoon sweat labor in the field. Not too far from the barrack, to the left was the almost duplicate one for female prisoners. God knows how many were in there and why they were kept in this part of the jungle. The guards and members of the management team stayed in the house facing both of the barracks, as if they were watching all the moves of us prisoners. This labor camp was located deep inside the valley thickened by jungles of trees, bamboo, and vines and surrounded by hills and mountains. Being in this part of jungle, one could never be sure if he could get out alive. We were faced with dangers all the time, ranging from wild beasts to diseases. Malaria and dysentery had claimed lives of some former prisoners. Escape from this labor camp was almost impossible. One could be shot to death by the guard if seen or caught running away! Even if one could get away into the jungle, one was more than likely to return to where he had started because the jungle was so thick with tall trees and vines that without a compass, disorientation was unavoidable.

By the end of my first day, when the warmth from the sun had dissipated into the evening, the whole space and the air of this part of the land became so isolated that I could feel and touch my loneliness. In the air, the birds were flying home to their nests, and the monkey cries echoed from faraway forests. I began to wonder what my wife and my boys were doing and if she knew that I had been moved to the labor camp. Through the grapevine, prisoners keep their hopes high, and also through rumors and the grapevine, we knew serving in the labor camp here in this locality was almost half the way home. I had hoped she would know I was there, and I was almost positive that her contact had informed her about me being here. Visitors were allowed to come for a short visit to bring in food supplements for their loved ones. One could not have imagined that in order to be able to buy food, tobacco, and medicine for their loved ones to bring them with them at each visit, they had to sell items such as clothes, jewelry, and heirlooms on the black market. In some cases, the metal roof on one's house was also among those items to be sold, piece by piece. Almost all visitors who came to see their relatives were on foot, walking a distance of fifteen to twenty kilometers with bags on their shoulders, in their hands, and most of all, with the eagerness to see their loved ones. Their love outweighed hardships of all forms, including ridicule from the government officials when they came to apply for a day pass for the visit. I wouldn't want my wife to go through all this trouble to come to see me here. It would be too much for her to handle. She had so much to do to keep our family going and to stay alive. I just hoped that our contact would help win my release early.

I was not asked to join the afternoon crew to work in the field; instead, I was given some items of food supplies such as rice, dried sweet potatoes, dried cassavas, and most importantly, sea salt. Those were our main foods during our stay; for the rest you were on your own, whether you got it from the field or from family visits. There were no kitchens and no dining halls in this camp. Everyone was to cook his own food the way he wanted over the fireplace that was fed with big trunks of trees at the middle of the camp. This was the only place that kept us warm and gave us a sense of being alive, for it constantly gave out glowing charcoal and smoke into the air.

At the end of the day, I came to join the workers who were coming back from the field to the little creek for washing and bathing. The water was clear and clean and always running; it must have come from those mountains, from the hills far away. It curved like a giant snake behind the tall grass bushes. The water was not deep; however, in some areas, one could drown easily, especially on the days with heavy rain. All the water from the mountains, from the hillsides, and from all over seemed to pour into this little stream, and it overflowed the banks. This creek did bring life to us in the evening when we got back from the field after a hardworking day in the hot sun. It always amused my friends and me, as we were told that we should pick our male washing spot at the upper stream to avoid the "contaminated" water downstream from where the girls washed. They believed that it would be unlucky to do so, as if there were something unluckier than being held in this labor camp.

My survival antenna was immediately put to work, as I had spotted some fish along the bushes. I was imagining a mud trout or a catfish on a stick over the glowing charcoal at the fireplace for dinner. It would be so delicious! And indeed, it wasn't before long I caught some of the nice-size healthy fish right there in the creek. I would use worms saved from working out in the field during the day and bait my lines in the evening. Very early in the morning I would check, and there was my dinner. Life began to get harder because the work load in the field—during the day, clearing the trees, preparing the soil for planting from corn to potatoes to cassavas, and in the evening, political meetings and self-confessions—would drain all of my energy. I and many other prisoners became physically weaker due to the lack of food and sleep. Wild veggies such as greens from bitter melon, dandelion, and leftover pieces of potatoes from previous harvests became rare survival commodities for all of us.

One day, a young fellow in our labor group saw a bunch of bananas that was turning yellow on the tree. He could not resist the craving, or he failed to dampen the temptation, or who knows if he had any clue of what the outcome would be if he picked it. Nevertheless, after he had that bunch of bananas down, it seemed like forbidden fruit from mystical garden. He hid it away, waiting to get a bite of it at the end of the working day. Unfortunately, a guard had passed by and noticed that the banana bunch was gone, and he went mad. He fired a couple shots into the air from his rifle and ordered the gathering of all prisoners next to the banana tree. This situation got to the point of being very serious, for he began to ask for voluntary admission of stealing of the bananas, his bananas, perhaps. The air was so thick and quiet that one could hear the cry of a monkey from far away in the woods. He looked at each of us who now sat on the ground motionless, wondering if he would actually kill someone for his bananas. His face turned from red to pale green, matching the color of his military fatigues. His eyes rolled back and forth as he pointed his rifle at each of us, screaming, demanding an answer. It seemed as if we all had a silent agreement that we would not point the finger at anyone, but we would let this madman discover the guilty one himself.

This young guard, who now had a gun in his hand, was probably tending cows in the field only months or weeks ago. He probably had very little education. But he was now given rights from the new government to have no respect for the elderly or for those whom he had previously served prior to the change of government. He could just pull the trigger on any one of us, and there was nothing anyone could do about it. A report from him labeling a person "reactionary" or "resistant" to the people's government was all that was needed, and his hands were washed clean. I had seen with my own eyes many dead on the road, many corpses decaying under the hot sun on my trail during the chaos days of evacuation out of my hometown, Cam Ranh. No one had had any time to care for or to bury the dead because they were concerned about the safety of their own. A stray mortar shell could land on one's roof, and a bullet could take one's life at any time.

A life of a Vietnamese person in this land was not as valued or as well treated as that of a pest in the civilized world. The war had not only taken its toll in terms of human lives but also had taken away the very chance for educational opportunities that would otherwise be available for many in this country. And that is why this man, with weapon in hand, a byproduct of a system that was lacking in education and the teaching of love and respect for one another, was acting like a mad, ruthless master over his slaves.

A search now began at the living quarters of all of our belongings for the stolen bananas. Every piece of bags, every corner of the barracks were checked and searched, and finally the yellow bananas were found at the young man's bag. The owner of the bag, after admitting the stealing, was immediately taken into the hut under the point of the rifle. We all in one way were relieved for not being tortured, but we were worried about what was going to happen to this young man; we all knew well that it was not going to be very pretty. As soon as the two of them entered the hut, we heard the moaning, the beating, and a few minutes later, the end of a drama came when the young man, with a bloody face, wobbled out through the door. The guard lifted himself up from behind, grabbing the bar over the front door with both of his hands and swung a kick with both of his feet at this man's back, which brought him facedown like a wounded animal, collapsed and flat on the ground, motionless.

The wind was gaining speed on this second-day morning, and the raindrops woke me up to the reality of a possible storm. Here and there prayers were heard over the wind. In the cabin, some concerns and worry were shown on the captain's face. What went on in his mind one would never know, but one could certainly bet that even though he was a seasoned fisherman who had many thousands of hours on the water, going through different phases of rough water, he had never been in this situation where his boat was laden with many lives bouncing with the waves. I had personally known this man for quite some time prior to this trip. We had shared many ideas and wishes for the future in the US. He had a very beautiful family, a wife and two daughters, who were also staying in the cabin with him. He had lately earned a lot of respect from the community for charting the course on two fishing boats that carried the families of his siblings, which successfully landed in the Philippines and confirmed their safe arrival via international Mailgram. For the past forty-eight hours he had showed his solid control over the maneuvering of the boat. The captain definitely looked tired but determined; he had a determination to bring this fishing craft to safety. Captain Ngoi, a man in his late thirties, a fair, dark-skinned good-looking man who didn't say much, but rather, always stayed behind the scenes. He must have had some connections with the authorities to gain his upper edge in obtaining special favors. I saw him in the cooking area at the Cam Ranh district jail after my release from the labor camp and wondered what in the world he was up to in there. Later on, I learned that he had been picked up and jailed for some past related political activities but was ready for a release thanks to his connection with Mr. Hoang, a high-ranking official in the police department who had helped many people, and I was one of them.

I was taken out of my jail cell by a guard one early afternoon in July 1976 for interrogation conducted by man in his civilian clothes who later on became Anh Hoang, brother Hoang to me. Hoang asked me to tell everything about the attempt and the escape in which I had been involved. Playing naïve and innocent, I told him I did not do anything and that I did not know what I was accused of and knew nothing about escaping. Hoang did not show any upset over my untruthfulness to him, and instead of any further questioning, he handed me a piece of paper that was folded in half, handwritten on both sides. In his soft voice he commanded me, "Read it."

At the very first glance at the handwriting on the paper, I immediately knew that it was my father-in-law's, and as I unfolded it, I read his statement of confession, in which I was named as involved in organizing an attempt to take our family and friends to cross the sea to the Philippines. And due to a flaw in the execution of our escape plan, we ended up in jail together. I was speechless and felt quite embarrassed, not knowing what to say, and quite frankly, I did not have courage to look at him, for I had lied to him earlier. I could not deny, nor could I ever be able to change the fact that was a statement written by my father-in-law in black and white. Time seemed to be standing still, and I could feel the weight, the uneasiness in the air. *What kind of punishment was I going to get?* I wondered. I had just been released from the concentration camp not too long before, and here I was, another jail time waiting for me.

"Write your own version of statement in as much detail as possible, describing what happened the best you can, and remember, the more honest, the sooner you will be going home," Hoang told me in his soft voice, serious but not threatening.

THE FIRST FAILED ATTEMPT

My father-in-law grew up in a coastal village called Tan An of Phan Rang province about forty-five miles south of the Cam Ranh Bay area. As a young boy he used to go fishing in the area, and as he was growing up, he left to go to school far away and seldom came back. As an adult, an appointed village chief, he came home more often and earned enormous respect from his extended family members and other villagers. Months after the war was over, he had made some contacts with his friends who owned sizable fishing boats in the village. At the end of his many months of contacts, he found two boat owners who would like to participate in our escape plan, which involved stocking a supply of food and fuel, all of which needed to be bought in minimum quantities on a daily basis and stored away at bushes by the shoreline. Arrangements were made for the boat owner's elderly parents, who decided to stay behind. They were to have some money to live on after everyone had left. All these monies and expenses came from fees we charged to a family friend, who lived in Saigon, who was also willing to advance the money to fund the entire operational expenses in exchange for seats on the boat.

And for us, we had no money left after we returned home from evacuation to Saigon and Vung Tau at the end of the war in 1975. In return, I had to risk getting caught and of course, suffer all the consequences such as jail time, labor camps, and possibly getting shot at to put this escape plan together. In order to have seats for everyone in the family, I saw no other way out of this trap except to engage myself in doing this so that my family could have a chance for a better life elsewhere. We had made arrangements with a local fisherman friend to taxi all of us in his boat to the two bigger ones and rendezvous outside of Cam Ranh Bay. A hefty fee was arranged for this service, for if anything went wrong, his boat and other properties would be confiscated, and jail cells would be waiting for him and his crew. It was a dangerous and risky job that required total trust from parties, my family and the boat owners, a well-thought-out plan, and ultimately, a flawless execution. In preparation for this exodus, many days and nights I had to travel to study the area—the trails, roads, swamps, and the creeks, all of which we would be passing by in the dark of the night. I wanted to make sure that we would get to where we wanted to go without any mistakes.

Family members and friends, one or two at a time, came and gathered at my place of residence one evening in the midsummer of 1977. At first they appeared and acted as visitors scattered in our backyard and the garden, which was rather spacious and fenced in. The idea of escape, crossing the sea, at that time was not in anyone's thinking; therefore no one would have ever paid any attention to any activities at my place. Later in the evening, after everyone was fed, they all quietly slipped away into hiding corners to avoid any unexpected visitors who might notice something unusual about our place, which might hinder or cause troubles for the execution of our plan. Traveling from one village to another required a day pass for all adults at this time in the south of Vietnam, and here I had people from as far as Saigon, more than three hundred miles away. Anyone caught here at my place would be a disaster to our operation, which involved months of planning in secret.

The first groups of our people were loaded on the evening bus, which was headed by one of our guys who knew where to have everyone get off and proceed through the route, heading to our meeting place. The second batch followed the very same procedures.

I was in the last group of twelve people getting off the bus when it was really dark. We took a very long walk, passing by the cemetery outside the village of Tan Binh, where we caught up with groups ahead of us right at the end of the burial place. It was also the beginning of the swamp where canoes and small boats were to be used to get all of us to the other side of water and wetland.

Kids were tired, hungry, and crying, and the adults tried to help ease their tantrums while others threatened their youngsters to shut up, all of which created a commotion, breaking the otherwise quiet of cemetery night. If someone in the village happened to peek out at this area at this moment of the night, he would probably think that he might have seen moving figures of ghosts. Or he might think that the dead had their gathering night. Nevertheless, after hours of paddling the boats, miles of walking, and weaving through the bushes, we got to the shoreline without incident. The sound of the waves breaking up at the beach, the cool fresh sea breeze, and the sight of thousands of lights out in the sea became refreshing elixirs for all of us. We were quite exhausted but happy getting to the finish line. We did not want to waste any time as we descended downhill toward the beach where we saw our taxi boat waiting, bouncing at each wave. This was the moment I had been waiting for. The night was so exquisitely beautiful. It must have been around midnight, and the sky was clear, filled with millions of twinkling stars. The smell of the salty seawater mingled with the sounds from the waves lapping the shore and the sides of the boat brought me all energy I needed to carry on my job.

The signal and the whispers from the boat owners to start boarding people onto the boats brought me back to reality. The ladies and children were helped onto the boat one at a time. I could see the line quickly shortening, and I was the last person to close the line getting onto the boat as it was being pushed away from the beach and out into the sea.

A few minutes out into the water as everyone was relaxing, enjoying the first and hardest part of their journey, I heard a high-pitched voice and many voices coming out from the back of the boat. It turned out that it was my father-in-law, who had discovered that his sons were not on the boat. The question was directed to me for an answer; at this point in time I had none. I was in a total shock that they were not among us on this boat, and I could not explain why to myself. I quickly did my mental checklist to see what had gone wrong. Did they show up at the location of the bushes where they were supposed to be for hiding? Did they patiently wait to join the group as we were going to be passing by? Had they been caught by the guards and taken away before we got there? Question after question, and I found myself numbed to have an answer. To make the matter worse, because I had no answers for myself, I had no explanation for him. His blame was all over me, and I became speechless and motionless.

My wife, who was holding my sons with her, tried to calm him down as she explained to him that whatever had happened, whatever the reason that her bothers were not here on the boat, it was not the end of the world; they could and they would find their way out. But he, in his moment of insanity, being hurt by not having his sons coming along and the notion that he was not going to be able to see them again, mercilessly shut her out by screaming at her, and she became quiet and sobbed uncontrollably.

The blaming, the screaming from my father-in-law tapered off into silence intermixed with words of consolation from our friends on the boat as we were waiting for the signals of the lights from the two boats that were supposedly coming for us. We were now about three miles off the shoreline, moving very slowly on the water, sometimes idling, trying to spot any signal coming from them. There were hundreds or thousands of lights from fishing boats twinkling on and off at the waves out in the vast sea. Which ones were supposed to be theirs? Our arrangement with the two boats was that we would see them between midnight and two in the morning. Lights flashed five times each at their arrival approximately two miles off the shoreline, and the two of them were to keep their distance not too far apart. If we did not see them during that two-hour time, we would have to assume that they were having trouble for whatever reason, be it from the family matters or from the local guards at their village, and that we would pull back and arrive home before daybreak to avoid any unpleasant surprises.

The deadline was approaching; there was emotional tension and internal pull among us on the boat. The majority would think, *Now, we have come this far. Let's be patient and wait a little longer; they will show up. The village where they come from is far away; it would take much longer time to travel on the water. There are myriad of potential problems that could make the boat unable to get here on time.* For my family, because of the absence of my brothers-in-law, I personally thought that I would never be happy and I would never hear the end of it. My vote was to turn the taxi boat around when the time was up, and that was what we did at about two in the morning; our taxi boat came to the spot where we took off hours earlier.

We got home without any trouble before dawn. Everyone was very tired physically and emotionally and went right to bed to catch up on their sleep. I was disappointed at the fact there was a flaw in carrying out our plan. The three brothers-in-law never left their bushes where they were waiting, but we missed them due to the homogeneity of the bushes in the dark; and they were all home now to tell their story of waiting.

I was too egotistically upset for all the blame and decided not to engage in this anymore. I was ready to throw in the towel when, at 10:00 a.m., my liaison arrived at the house to inform that the two boats had arrived and were now waiting out in the water. I told my friends that I had made up my mind that I quit. Now that the boats were here, anyone who desired to go would be on his own. I relinquished my role of leader and organizer of the escaping business. I felt very tired.

At noontime, however, my friend's mom and his family asked me to reconsider my decision, for they had risked everything to come this far, and the boats were there ready to go. They certainly did not want go back to Saigon, where they would find their house all empty and surely confiscated by the government, and jail was certainly waiting for them.

"For our friend's sake and for our family's sake, please do it again," pleaded my wife. I was giving it lots of thought, especially because of the situation my friend and his family were in. They had left everything behind and had come this far to depend on me to get them out, to go together with us. I now began to see my moral obligation to go to the finish line. I then agreed to it and turned that machinery in motion as I assigned the contact to the boats and told them that they should not leave the spot where they were. I also wanted to make sure that the boys would be included into the moving body so that they would not be left out again.

That put a smile on everyone's face, and the plan was on. I had to take care of the welfare, the livelihood of my friends and other people who came to work with me to make this happen. I felt guilty when I abandoned them. I swallowed my pride and crushed my ego.

The very same procedures were to be repeated the following night with extra precautions, for the rumors had traveled throughout the village that there was a commotion at the cemetery the night before, which appeared to be ghost-like activities. We needed to be very careful this time because I was very sure that the Communist intelligence network would pick up the rumors as well, and besides, they didn't believe in the supernatural and ghost stories. That would mean there were going to be more patrols on the field.

After crossing the swamps, passing through the woods and bushes, about three-quarters of the way to the shoreline, we were suddenly stopped, and the line of moving people became motionless, except that the signal from the people at the front line whispered back that all needed to be very quiet. Everyone in the line was taking a break from a rather long walk by sitting down. I quickly moved to the front of the line to see what had happened. I had sensed something was not going right but was not sure what until I talked to the scouting persons who were coming back from their checking.

"The beach is full of patrol guards," whispered one of the two scouts.

"We need to pull back," said the other.

At this new revelation and devastating news, we had no choice, no option, other than to return home. I knew for sure that my friend and those on the two boats had also discovered that the cops were roaming the beach and they had to take off without us. I asked everyone to follow the same route heading back, and to his or her home they should go. At this point I could not promise anything, could not say anything except to encourage them to be very careful so as not to get caught on their way returning home and that we should meet again for the next one.

As soon as I safely got home, after hours with my wife and my boys on a tiny canoe-like boat, moving quietly along the banks of the river, weaving by the edge of the village, I decided to head out on my Honda motorcycle to the rice field by the foot of a mountain about ten kilometers north of our house to work and to find my quiet time as much as to avoid a possible raid from the government at our home.

While I was lying under the shade of the tree, relaxing and pondering on the things that had gone wrong and mentally going back step by step, bush by bush, I asked myself this question: What could have been done to avoid the fiasco in the past two intensive, hectic days? While I was away at the rice field, the cops from the district headquarters had come to search at our house, and my father-in-law was handcuffed and taken away.

When I got home late in the evening, thinking that I was going have a nice dinner and a good night's sleep after that, the cop was waiting for me with handcuffs. What I did not know was those relatives and companions who traveled back to their homes after leaving our place were stopped at the checkpoint at the borderline between the two cities of Cam Ranh and Phan Rang, and since they did not have day passes, they were pulled off the bus for questioning. My name, my plan of escape, and my place of residence were noted in their confession, and the result was a prison cell again.

The sea was getting rougher every minute as the wind gained speed; the waves seemed like multiple tongues of death ready to swallow my little boat that was bouncing, gliding from one wave to another. The water was no longer peaceful blue. Now the bubbles foamed at each crash between waves. The sky was gloomy with dark clouds moving low over our heads, ready to dump more water onto us. Every now and then, despite skillful maneuvering from the boat captain to keep this little fishing craft afloat, the water still splashed into the boat, scaring the soul out of every one of us who was not used to rough sea life. Only a few fishermen were calm and agile and quickly emptied the water out from the boat before the next splash of water got into it again. The rainwater coming down from the above and the water splashes from the sea and the strong wind could not help but to worsen the feeling of the already half-soaked people packed like sardines at the bottom of the boat. All this compounded to heighten the worries of their fate; the chill from the cold weather and the chilling thoughts of becoming food for sharks bound them tighter for physical warmth and comfort. I did not hear anyone say, "If I knew that this was my destiny, this was my way of facing my death, I would not have come on this boat." There were no complaints; instead, the faith, the prayers mumbling from the mouths of Christian and Buddhists alike to their gods mingled with the angry roars of the sea and thunder and lightning.

In this very moment I could not help but think of an experience in which I was trapped under the water during one of my fishing trips not too far from the shoreline. During my learning to become a seasoned fisherman to be capable of handling the out-of-the-ordinary of the sea, I was always alone, learning the characteristics of the sea such as tides ebbing and how it affected fishing. In one incident, I was under the water, and I wanted to move a bamboo fish trap into a spot where lots of logs and branches had accumulated at the bottom of the water. It was a perfect spot for all kinds of fish to play and to feed. Because of the time it took to move the trap and to hide it in a spot where it became a part of the natural habitat of the fish, I ran out of oxygen in my own gas tank. My lungs demanded air and oxygen as my hands and my body tried to wiggle their way out and up to the surface. I had gulped lots of water as I was fighting for air. I continued to struggle my way up. The thought of death under the water in the sea and with no one knowing about it, and the idea that I would become food for the fish, propelled me to push myself harder and harder. The surface of the water seemed so remote. The air was not within my reach as my head and my whole body were struggling, fighting, shaking for air; the commodity at this moment that defined life and death and was the very thing that had been taken for granted. At last, as a miracle of many miracles of my life, the faint light of the sky above the water appeared clearer, and the last few strokes of my feet pushed me up out of the water. I was completely exhausted when I surfaced. This thought was somehow coming back to me in this situation. The smell of the seawater and the taste of it in my mouth, along with the chill of the wind and the sound of the waves crashing upon one another in the sea, and the rain coming down from the above, pushed me back to the moments of the past incident when life and death were as close as a thought.

"She is having contractions," someone screamed out from the big, open hole at the middle of the boat. There was lots of noise from those who were yelling for help as the mother-to-be was in pain with her contractions.

I was thinking to myself that this was not a very good time to be born, baby! I was silently telling the unborn, "While we are struggling between life and death on this boat in the sea, you decide to join us in this battle for life. I don't think this is a good idea, nor do I think this is a good time for your worldly venture either. So could you just hold on? Could you just delay until we get to the shoreline, to the harbor, where it is safer for you and your mother? But if you do, as your destiny, have to come, hopefully you will bring us good fortune and safe arrival." As I was mentally conversing with the unborn, the mother was moaning in pain and was ready to deliver any minute. We all panicked!

The question became urgent as to who would deliver her baby. Almost everyone, mostly the ladies, was either seasick or not brave enough to take on this task in these weather conditions in which we were all wet and unable to move as the boat was being bounced at each wave. A few good men of us would not have anything to offer on this task, and I felt helpless. It became critical, as it would become a disaster if no one helped her. Each time she moaned in pain, signaling the urgency for help, I could not help but ask my wife, who was also under the weather, seasick, to give some help, even though she had never been a midwife.

After seconds of hesitation, she crawled toward the mother and minutes later, delivered her baby. It was a boy! She cried out as the boy cried his first cry, which mingled with and faded into the roars of the sea in the middle of nowhere on this vast, troubled water. The cord was cut with a pair of scissors, the only tool besides a knife that was available on the boat. It was stained with rainwater and not at all sterilized. She had no other choice! She did with what she had to save the lives of the mother and her son. We gave her lots of credit for her performance! I did not know if I silently said to him, "Son, welcome into the troubled world on this boat."

Anyhow, we had just added one more body, one more person, to the headcount of the group, which was yet to be determined. The baby was wrapped with a towel and with his mom, was tucked away in the bottom corner of the boat, where it was warmer, with the hope that they were going to make it until we got to land.

We must have been on the water for the third straight day. The boat had now stopped moving, and the engine was no longer making noises. All of this happened because the wind reduced its racing speed, and the captain decided to change the oil to make sure that the engine had a little time off to rest and to receive proper care and maintenance so that it could continue its mission to bring this fishing craft to its final destination, the Philippine shoreline. I wondered how many miles we had been on the water. No one could tell because we had no tools, no gadgets to keep track of the distance we had traveled. A little compass was all we had to keep us in the right direction, but the wind and the storm pushed us far off from where we should have been. God only knew where about on this vast water we were. As the boat was bouncing with the waves and drifting to the wind, my mind also drifted away into a past incident in which the Communists were very close to catching me.

In Dong Ba Thin, there was a former Special Forces Training Center for the US and Vietnamese military special operations personnel, whose main duty was to fly in Cambodian soldiers to receive training and then to fly them back home to Cambodia after graduation. At present it was occupied by the regimental headquarters of North Vietnamese Army (NVA), whose troops were, instead of engaging in combat operations, involved in the agricultural production, mainly salt farming and growing vegetables. The soldiers from this unit were seen every day in their white T-shirts and moss green khaki trousers, lined up row after row in front of the main building, doing their physical exercises. After that, they were sent to the fields for farming or to the salt farm along the water line inside the Cam Ranh peninsula. This military installation was about a quarter of a mile off the road, the main highway, numbered one, connecting Saigon, Cam Ranh, Nha Trang, and many cities to the north. Its entrance faced the east, or the sea. Close to it were salt farms. I happened to come in contact with a former coworker by accident. This fellow was a friend who used to work for Cam Ranh Bay fire department as hose man and firefighter, named Lime. He was a trustworthy guy in his early thirties. Like many other friends and acquaintances who disappeared after the war was over for many reasons beyond their control, some were driven to start their lives in new economy zones in the jungle, while others were sent to concentration, re-education camps.

One afternoon, I was out walking; the sun was high, and the breeze was just enough to cool off the July heat mixed with the smell of mud and salt from the salt farms. Here and there, a few birds chirped in the nearby bushes, as if signaling an unexpected welcome as I was walking, exploring and investigating the area of salt farms for possible route of escape. I discovered a thatched-roof hut built on four poles, of which two were on the ground and the others were in the water of what seemed like a fishpond. It was kind of quiet early in the afternoon, a siesta, perhaps, for those who worked and stayed here during the day. As I came closer to the hut, perhaps because of me making some noise as I was walking, or perhaps because of the charge in the air that drew the man inside the hut to come out, I immediately recognized that young man as an old friend. After moments of happy surprise at seeing each other, we went inside the hut and told each other stories of the old days as well as the new ones of this difficult time under the new rules. I was very careful not to let him know my intentions until weeks later.

After many visits to his place, getting to know him and his wife, making sure that they were still friends in good terms, I told them my plans and my intention of using his facility to hide people during the day and that all would travel across the river when the night came. He agreed to it with one and only one condition—that he and his wife would be included in the group. He was happy to be a part of our planning as well as an essential and a facilitating person as well. He loved my ideas of having people in groups of three or less dressed in farming outfits arrive at his place very early in the morning as if going to work or to purchase salt and then one by one disappear into his hut. This plan would work for the adults, but to hold kids in this hut for a day would be almost impossible. The solution to this was to drug them, make them sleep all day and all night, if needed.

After weeks of planning, studying the terrain, and investigating the activity patterns of soldiers from the nearby headquarters, we decided to launch our escape from this very location simply because there were no villagers and no cops around. The uniformed soldiers had their own schedules and activities, and after their workdays, one could very be certain that they were inside their compound. So if we worked around their time schedule, we were pretty sure that we could avoid almost all surprises.

D-day came in the midsummer; the boat was scheduled to be out waiting at the shoreline by the beach. I became a Communist soldier, complete with light moss green khaki uniform that I had purchased on the black market. I walked around the area of the hut, making sure that it was safe and that my people were coming in, and then disappeared into the hut as planned. My wife and my children, Lam and Tuan, had come earlier in the morning and were inside the hut. By sunrise, the job of hiding people was well executed, and all nervousness evaporated with the daylight. I checked in with my guys at the hut every now and then to let them know everything seemed to be going well for all of us and that they needed to be patient, resting and waiting for a long night ahead, as we were going to cross the river by a small boat a few persons at a time, and then all of us were to walk at least two miles of jungle to the sea beach, where the boat would come to fetch us away.

Unfortunately, and unexpectedly, at about 9:00 a.m, after everything seemed to be quiet and well going, as I was walking in the field as a soldier, pretending to be on a mission of checking in the field, I noticed that there was a group of people emerging from the river about half a mile north of our hut. This group of people—heaven knows where they came from—appeared to be men and women and children, some carrying babies, some dragging their younger ones. Their clothes were torn in pieces, and they were wearing no shoes, limping toward me as I was trying to close the gap between us. I also noticed that there were bloody scratches all over their legs and arms, some on their faces. They were frightened and very tired. I approached them without realizing that I was a Communist soldier in uniform that made them very scared. They definitely were afraid that I might put handcuffs on them and send them to prison. And on the other hand, I myself was also afraid that this situation could get my people and me in a very deep trouble. And for me, if got caught in this uniform, my life would be forever doomed. But before I was able to ask them or say anything, a rather aged lady who must have been the mother and grandma of the group came forward, her hands in the prayer position, bowed down her head, and begged me not to put her and her family in jail. She said her family was taken to the jungle to the other side of the river and told to wait nearby the shoreline for a boat to come to pick them up. But after more than two weeks of waiting, hungry and thirsty, no one showed up as promised. They realized they were all victims of a scam in which they gave money to buy their seats on a boat, but they never saw the boat; nor did they ever see those who gave them the promise. How brutal and how inhumane and how sad! There was always someone who could care less about your well-being but take your money.

I had no time to ask and to explain anything except that I wanted to show my empathy and to get them out of this area as quickly as I possibly could.

"I am a soldier," I said to them. "I do not want to put you all in jail. But all you need to do is to go straight to the road, avoiding the military post, and then catch the bus before the cops come."

As they were limping off to the road, I was pondering on the thought that if these people got caught on the bus or before getting on the bus, the chances were that the real soldiers and real cops would come to check this area out, and we all were going to be in trouble. I had no time to think any further. I could not afford to see my wife, my children, and my friends being handcuffed to the jail cell, and I, being caught in their uniform, was just sure a death sentence would await me! I looked at those poor people getting close to the road and immediately went into the hut to let everyone know the gravity of the situation and that everyone needed to find their own way home. After everyone left the hut, walking out in many directions, I hurriedly took my family onto a little rowboat that had been pulled off to the ground down the river and headed upstream at full speed to another village before any unpleasant surprises could befall us. At first, it appeared to be a little hectic, a little chaotic, for fear of encountering cops who might be in the area because of the commotion from the failed attempt. At last I was able to get all of us into the boat, and off we went. It took me a little while to get my emotions under control and to manage the boat, keeping it in balance, and after getting a good distance from the hut, I felt the danger was over. Despite the fallout, it sure felt like a little picnic, a leisure time for my family that would never otherwise have happened. It was just a beautiful morning; the sky was light blue with a few patches of white clouds lazily drifting away to the sea. The sounds of a few birds chirping and flying off from one tree to the other along the river made this part of the morning quite pleasant, and it seemed that all troubles had dissipated away. We were all so quiet that we must have been absorbing the soothing beauty of the nature, and at the same time, we felt that any noise, any talking, might draw attention from any passerby. However, my mind was on the plan for the next move.

"Where are we? How many more kilometers before we get to the shoreline?" someone asked the boat captain.

"Don't know. Just keep on going. Hopefully in the next five or ten hours or next day we will get there," he said perfunctorily.

I knew that he was just guessing, and his was just as good as anyone else's on this boat, for he did not even know where about on this surface of water we were. The only thing he and anyone could do was to keep moving. Hopefully we all would get there or anywhere there was solid land.

Now that the oil changing was done and the boat was keeping its course to the east, we assumed we were heading to the Philippine Islands. The sky was dark, full of clouds flying very low above us, promising more rain to be on the way. I silently prayed that the wind would not be as violent as it had been in the last two days, at least until we found a shoreline. The wind, the waves, and the rain were a terrifying and deadly mix for all of us on this fragile wooden craft that had been miraculously holding on its own despite the weight it was carrying. It must have been very heavy because I could touch the water with my hand from the boat. There must have been many thousands of kilos of human bodies that were now scattered into every corner, covering every inch inside the boat. Despite the abusive waves slapping her sides, despite the intrusive waves climbing into the boat, she seemed to be proud and faithful and protective of all of us so far.

How much longer, how much farther could she, an old fishing craft, keep afloat, was the question she did not know the answer to, nor did anyone among us. We were thankful for being alive and safe thus far. Who knew what would happen tomorrow and the day after tomorrow? I instinctively believed that despite all hardships and despite all risks and dangers, somewhere, some-how, I would always miraculously be saved.

During my high school years, one evening after dinner I was asked to come along with friends to visit a blind fortuneteller, a sort of a psychic. Upon entering the house with a thatched roof and dirt floor, I saw a lady in her early fifties sitting on her bed; next to it was a small table. The light from the oil lamp was enough for me to cast my first glance at her face as I bowed to utter my respectful greeting to her. I immediately noticed that she had lost her sight, whether from birth or from an accident or from whatever other causes, I would never know. Both her eyes were closed shut, but her voice was clear and soothing. She had an aura of a good mother and a kindness about her. Every one of us had a chance to talk to her and to ask her questions about our past and future based on our birthdate. All of us did agree later that her fortune telling was fairly accurate, but what seemed to be an extra on my part was, as she told me, I had a very poor, unloving childhood (my mom passed away, and my father remar-ried), and sometimes I was in danger. But there was a lady, or perhaps a lady spirit, who was always around me to guide me and to protect me from harm.

As we left the fortuneteller's house after paying for her ser-vice, I pondered on what I was told about my female guardian spirit. I now believed that the spirit or the soul that saved me from dangers many a time was that of my own mother, who left me when I was only seven years of age. And yes, there had been numerous incidents and events that I had encountered in my lifetime that would need miracles to explain and miracles to get me through. One such an incident was that of my military service experiences at camp A 232, a Special Forces installation at Tan Rai of Bao Loc, Lam Dong province, in which a few incoming enemy artillery shells landed inside our military compound and exploded yards away from our bunker where I was standing, sending dirt, debris, shrapnel, and dust all over our compound. There were no casualties, and I escaped the death of that incident by a miracle. Not long after that incident that almost took my life, my commander, Captain Striler, one evening outside of the camp headquarters, looked at me and said, "Sam, you are too young to get killed over here. Why don't you get your ass out of here tomorrow, okay?"

"Yes, sir," I said. The following day, off on a helicopter, I was flown to B23, USSF headquarters, located in the heart of Ban Me Thuot City, where it was safe. From there I was last deployed with B51, the Special Forces of Dong Ba Thin training center in the Cam Ranh area. Her spirit was watching over me then and throughout my military career. I had participated in countless operations, patrols, FTXs (field training exercise), and sometimes I took part in joint operations of US, Vietnamese, ROK (Republic of Korea). I climbed mountain after mountain, hill after hill. My feet had measured hundreds of miles of jungles and creeks. I never ever had to pull the trigger. The spirit of my mother, I had come to believe, must have shielded me from the enemy lines so that during all those years of hostile activities, I had not had any contact with the Charlie (VC). Now I had every reason to believe that she was here in this unpleasant, threatening weather to protect my family and me.

Rain and wind had resumed as predicted, as our boat had been on this journey for the fourth day. Rain poured down on us more than enough water to drink and too much for us to stay warm. Since I was on the deck with my sons and my wife, all of whom were soaking wet and cold, I could feel the rain slap my face every time the wind blew. I could more so feel the pain of being helpless. I felt sorry for them, especially my very young children, who had never been exposed to this lengthy harsh weather. The color of their faces and their lips had turned darker, and their bodies shivered at times under the rain, which pierced and tormented my heart. What could a father do to keep his children warm in this situation and most importantly, to keep them from getting sick? The thought of them getting colds and pneumonia right here on this boat was just as painful as something wrenching my heart. A piece of six-by-six white plastic sheeting that I had brought along for our family to use in this particular situation had been used as an SOS flag on the first day of the storm. It got damaged and torn to pieces by the wind and was disposed of into the sea, and now we were completely exposed to the rain.

I needed to be creative and do something very quickly before things got worse for my children. Everything we had was all soaking wet either with rainwater or from the sea splashes. I decided to create a roof for us using my only towel, which was also soaked with water. I began lying on my back, each of my arms curved up in the air, having each of my sons lying close next to me and my hands in an upward position, holding tight to each corner of the towel, and my feet would grip the other end corner of the towel. It was sort of a mini tent for my boys and me under the slanted roof of my towel. It did help run the rainwater off to my feet and kept us from getting any wetter. Besides, I was able to keep my boys warm with the heat of my own body, and gradually the three of us survived the rain and the cold. And I was happy that my boys were all warmed up afterward and the healthy color had returned to the skin of their faces.

Later in the afternoon, the rain subsided and the boat captain announced that he needed to quiet the engine so that he could put some more fuel into the tank. He then discovered that there was only one five-gallon can left, and no one had any idea where we were and how much longer this can of diesel would last and how much farther it would take us. The fuel was poured into the tank; the off-white-colored empty plastic can was then tossed into the water. It bounced in the waves for a few minutes, and the wind pushed it away. It quickly disappeared into the immensity of the sea. I wished that they had not let go of that can, for who knew that it might save one of our lives? Now we knew we had somewhere fewer than ten gallons of fuel to take this boat to our destination or any shoreline. And how far was it from here? Would it make it there? I am very sure these questions were popping up in everyone's heads, but no one wanted to say them out loud. Everyone wanted to keep this worry and anxiety to themselves. As one of the organizers of the group, I would not allow myself to display any sign of worry on my face or in my behavior, even though, at seeing the empty fuel can drifting and fading away into the other end of water, a little of my faith was shaken and some of my hope had also gone with that empty can.

The engine now became alive, and the boat was moving east at its normal speed, as if it were in a fuel-saving mode. Whether it was the intention of the boat captain or not, I felt that we needed to consume as little fuel as we could possibly could, for no one knew how much longer before we hit the land or we hit the storm. Indeed, in front of us a rather large, dark cloud appeared drifting toward us. We were wondering if this could be another storm coming our direction. We would be devastated in the situation in which we might not have enough fuel to keep the boat straight, facing the wind. If that were the case, this would be the last of our journey. Immediately we realized that we had no choice, nor did we have any option other than to continue our course of direction. Whatever came, whether it was a typhoon or the storm, we would deal with it head-on with courage and prayers.

Just about an hour or so later, as the distance between our boat and the dark cloud of storm got shorter, I did not know which one was moving faster, our boat or the cloud. It became a little vague at first, as our eyes were fixing on the block of the dark cloud. It did not seem to be moving, and we were approaching it closer and closer. It turned out to be something we had been all praying for, longing for: a shoreline, an island! We all were so very happy. Just minutes ago we were afraid that we would be facing a storm, and now, we were overjoyed that it was an island. We knew that we were saved; we could not help but look at each other and scream with joy. Yes, it was indeed a virgin island as we came closer and discovered that there were no humans living on this island. *Is this island a part of many islands of the Philippines?* we wondered. None of us had any clue.

When our boat actually came close to touching the island, we found out that we had neither ropes nor anchors, for all had been tossed away at the beginning of our journey. Some of the crew-members decided to lighten our load by letting go of their tools. Maybe they did not know of their importance. Either way, it was the biggest mistake a seaman could make while at sea because he must have them to keep his vessel in line with the wind, espe-cially in the storm, to prevent it from being capsized. Now that we were on an anchorless boat, I had to figure out how and what to use to hold my boat down. I was thinking and began to realize that the seawater was now blue again and it was peaceful and safe where we were behind the island.

The trees and plants on the island were so green, and their leaves were lustrously wet after the rainfall. There were small streams of water curving their way down from the hill, merging into the seawater. I could see the soil was humus as if it were well organically fertilized for vegetation. All of these colors gave me the sense of being alive, of surviving and stability, unlike the feel-ing of uncertainty we had just an hour or so ago, when we were surrounded by waves, crashing, bouncing, and the fuel was low, and the boat might stop moving any time, as well as the possibil-ity that the boat might capsize. One's imagination could stretch far to the worst scenario that could have happened to all of us. I wished, at this moment of relief, that I could stretch my arms long enough to wrap them around the island and give it a hug.

Nevertheless, I was standing up stretching myself at the very front of the boat, observing as well as absorbing the new scen-ery around us. Far away to the other side of this island, there was another island and a cluster of islands. This new discovery brought me a feeling of gratitude, and I was in awe that somehow we were being guided to land at the heart of these many islands. And as if adding to our good fortune, I exclaimed with joy when we discovered from far away that there was a very small fishing boat coming toward us, and whoever and whatever it was, we were definitely safer now to discover other human beings being around us. This news was joyfully shared among every one of us as that boat was heading toward our direction. He must have spotted our boat as I spotted his. When I saw him just about a hundred yards or so from our boat, I could not help but go crazy as I jumped into the water with my shorts and swam to his boat. I did not care if anyone on my boat would think about me as being nuts, crazy, or out of my mind.

Honestly, I did not have time for that; all I wanted was to be able to communicate with that lone fisherman on his tiny boat. I wanted to know who he was, where on earth we were, and what country he was from, or what country we were in. Did it matter anymore where we were or what nationality this fisherman was? I knew in my heart that I came to him to get help, and that was why I wanted to be in contact with him.

As soon as I climbed on his boat, which had a canoe-like shape with two bamboo riggers on either side to keep the boat balanced in unfriendly weather, I found the man to be a Filipino fisherman with a kindhearted smile on his face. He turned off his gasoline engine, which was mounted at the back of his boat with a long shaft that drove the propeller. I told him that I was a Vietnamese who escaped from Vietnam and my companions and I were seeking refuge in the US naval base in the Philippines. There seemed to be a language barrier in our communication. However, thanks to sign and body language, we got along just fine. We started out with his invitation to me asking me if I was any hungry and if I would like to have some rice that he had left over in his rice cooker. My eyes caught sight of the small, uncovered pot, which was half-full of white rice, as he pointed at it. It was the best rice I had had in days. He understood that we were from Vietnam and that we were interested in going to the US bases in the Philippines. He indicated that bad weather or a storm was coming to the region and that he would like to guide us to his village where the Philippine naval base was also located. He asked me also to tell my boat captain to follow his boat, which I did, and I also told my wife and the rest of my companions that I would like to stay with his boat just in case any communication and instructions were needed so I was there to act accordingly. As soon as instructions were clearly conveyed to the captain and all on my boat, the Filipino fisherman and I, on his fishing boat, took the lead, and the captain immediately followed behind.

TYPHOON HITS AND
FAMILY IS LOST

Just a few minutes later, as we moved away from the island, the center of the typhoon, or storm, arrived, hitting us with wind and rain so hard that we were completely covered with blankets of water. It felt like heaven had just released high-water-pressure pipes upon us. I could not see my boat anymore. It was just a thick sheet of water blowing in the wind. I asked the fisherman to turn his boat around so that I could find my boat. His answer was blunt and cold without a bit of sympathy for me, for my family, and for my companions on that boat. He, perhaps, was very scared of the storm and worried about his own safety.

"No, no, no more gasoline," he said, and on he continued his course to his village, his home. What happened to my boat, I had no clue. I could picture the whole scenario of what could have happened in those very short few minutes. As we were leaving the island, the center of the typhoon hit us; the wind was so strong, so violent, combined with heavy rain that was blowing the side of the big boat. Since it was not equipped with any balancers like those on the fisherman's boat, it might have capsized unless the captain was fast enough to make a quick turn to have his boat flowing with the wind; then his boat could have been saved.

The reality was that the fisherman and I were soaking wet

under the storm on his boat, which was shaking in the wind, bouncing in and with the waves. But thanks to the riggers on both sides of his boat, it kept on moving. I was helpless and hopelessly sitting in the middle of his boat, letting him take me wherever he wanted to. I was just completely devastated at the fact that I had been with my wife and my sons all along since I left Vietnam, and now, at the end of our journey, I had lost them. Here I was, utterly at his mercy. He must have operated his boat instinctively, for I could see nothing but a wall of rainwater coming down, which slapped my face with strong wind. The boat was shaking violently at each wave, and all I could barely see were white splashes of seawater hitting the sides of the boat. Finally he managed to bring his boat safely to the dock, which had some sort of a roof covering it. There was an electric light that showed the rain threads coming down heavily like flakes of the snow at the spotlight. As soon as I got off the boat and stood myself on the dock under the cover, the village chief, Mr. Miguel, a healthy, well-built man in his late forties, came to receive me in his military raincoat and immediately greeted me.

After hearing my story of how I had lost my people, he sent for the commander of the Philippine naval base nearby, and within minutes, the uniformed navy commander arrived. Both of the men tried to comfort me, but in no way were they able to help me in this situation. The commander told me, "Mr. Le, if anything happened, it has happened already. I could not send any of my men out to look for your people. It is too dark. It is too dangerous to go out in this stormy weather."

At that, I felt the last drop of my hope that the navy might find my people evaporate with the wind, and I became a hopeless, lonely man in a foreign land. The storm was defeating me. The chief then took me to his house, where his wife and his two beautiful daughters warmly greeted me. Everyone was at their best, trying to comfort me. The chief let me use his clothes and asked me to join his family for dinner, at which time I poured out my stories and the story of my escape. Everyone felt sorry for me and said they would pray for my family and hope for the best for them out there.

After dinner, I spent my quiet time in the kitchen, where there was a firewood stove burning to warm my body and my soul. I began to sob uncontrollably as I remembered the faces of my wife and those of my sons, their smiles, and their laughter. They were with me just hours ago and now were gone. What happened to them? Were they safe? Where were they at that moment? Were they cold and hungry? Question upon question, and no one could give me answers. I should not have left them. I should have stayed on that boat with them so that if death were the thing to come, I would die with them. I was blaming myself. My heart was now heavy with sorrow. I prayed for their safety and envisioned the boat not capsized but floating with the wind to safety of land or anywhere that was safe for all of them.

Later in the night, the storm got stronger and stronger every minute. The house was literally shaking at each strong gust blowing from all directions. The trees were falling down, sending destructive sounds throughout the village. The chief came to check on me to make sure that I was holding up okay and to tell me that it was the worst storm since 1947 in this island of the Philippines. This news, along with the sound of the wind beating against the house, just heightened my worries for my family and everyone on that boat out there in the rain. My prayers inside me for the peace and safety of my people and my boat seemed mingled with the sounds of the wind and the rain slapping against the wall of the house and the howling of the storm every time the wind picked up speed.

The morning came with not-so-good news, as the weather forecast predicted a lengthy storm that meant no one would be able to do a search-and-rescue mission, at least for today. The hosting family was quite marvelous. They cared for me physically and emotionally. They made sure that I had to eat well with them, three meals a day. They comforted me every now and then, making sure that my hopes and my spirits were always high and alive. I spent most of my time in the kitchen, where there was firewood burning all the time. It was where I warmed myself not only with the heat from the burning wood, but the memories, reflections, meditations, and the kindness of the members of this household.

This reminded me of an incident when we were on our way to visit my family in Ban Me Thuot of the central highland. A friend of my in-laws offered us a ride but did not know exactly where my parents lived. He just knew the general area of the city, where he used to do business. He was in the business of trucking and hauling lumber. When we arrived at the city after almost a day on the road—and it was getting late in the evening—instead of staying in the city, he was nice enough to take us to our remote village. As he turned his truck to go on a small road to our home, he realized that it was just a dirt road and a very narrow one. The way he asked questions concerning the distance and safety of the road, I could sense that he did not really want to go all the way to the village as he had promised. It was getting dark quickly because the hills and mountains surrounded the area, and the dirt road was flanked with trees and bushes. His was the only vehicle on the road. It was a 2I/2-ton diesel truck, and it sounded very much like a military vehicle moving in the dark. He was scared and felt very uneasy as time went on. He was afraid his truck might get shot at or blown up because it was in wartime. An ambush, the snipers, anything could happen. About two-thirds of the way, he really chickened out and decided to drop us off at the church at the village nearby on the left-hand side of the road. As soon as we had our luggage off his truck, he said good-bye and hurried his way back out to the city. We, a young couple with two little boys, Lam and my youngest son, Tuan, only eight months old, were in front of the church. We knew no one in this village; we were literally abandoned in the dark. The mountainous climate brought evening chills to all of us who had suddenly become helpless. The church had already closed its doors; we were only couple of kilometers away from home but in no way able to walk home with the belongings and the children.

At this distressful moment, a middle-aged couple came by, seemingly from nowhere. After they found out that we were dumped off and had no place to stay overnight, they took us to their home, fed us, and made sure that we were well taken care of before we got on the road again next morning. That very night my little baby was not feeling well. Maybe because he felt he was in an unfamiliar place that brought on his discomfort, he just cried and cried his heart out. The lady of the house told us that he must have an abdominal cold or some sort of stomachache based on her observation about his crying and his moving of his body. I believed she must have had many kids of her own in order for her to have this kind of knowledge. She then quickly applied some kind of ointment or balm of her own to his tummy and kept his stomach area warm, and in just a few minutes, my son Tuan was all better and fell asleep. We were so grateful for their kindness, for they opened the doors of their house and the doors to their heart to welcome us in. Today, many years later, in a different country more than a thousand miles away, I was in someone else's house, full of caring and kindness and warmth. I am so grateful to all of them.

The day seemed longer for me as the storm of unmerciful wind and rain continued its course, howling, beating violently against the houses, the trees, the plants. I could see the banana trees by the side of the house, whose branches with broad leaves got hit very hard and had already collapsed, hanging down against the tree trunk as if holding on to it to give it protection even though the wind, every few minutes, tried to strip them away, making them swing back and forth and sometimes swinging around the trees. The banana tree trunks themselves in their mixed colors of light green and light brown seemed to be steadfast in holding on their own upright position, not letting go of the branches as if saying, "Hold on."

Every inch of the front and backyard was covered with broken branches; leaves in different colors—green, yellow, amber, and burgundy—were pasted on the ground. The giant tree with a large canopy of branches broke down, leaving its limbs scattered all over the garden in the front of the house. What a messy, destructive scenery Mother Nature had created in this part of the country! *How many houses were there*, I wondered, *whose roofs were damaged and blown off in the wind last night? How many people—men, women, children, and babies—were frightened and cried in the cold last night?*

The chief went out to check on his villagers very early that morning and was not back yet. He was probably taking his time comforting his people whose houses and properties were damaged by the storm. Or perhaps he was at the naval base conferring with the officers as well as checking on possibilities of a rescue mission of my boat people who were out there in the boat in the wind. I hoped and prayed that they were hanging on to it until I came to get them. They must have been very hungry because no one could cook food in this weather. They must survive on dry or dehydrated goods they brought from home. I just hoped that they all stayed dry by all means so that they did not get sick or even caught pneumonia. Oh Lord, there was so much I worried about them. I prayed for God to please have mercy on them. I wanted them alive when I came to get them.

The day was almost over. There was no sign of the storm letting up. The village was lifeless. The streets were empty, except every now and then the leaves and debris were blown, skidding off the ground for a couple of feet and then staying motionless until the next batch of the wind came along. The people and animals stayed inside their houses and hutches. The only sign of life was the smoke from their kitchens, which escaped out from under the thatched roofs. I could imagine that in each household all the family members were gathering together and enjoying the warmth of the firewood burning with amber charcoal, and adding to it were the cracking sounds of the wood burning and the flame flickering. I hoped and prayed that I could find my family soon, perhaps tomorrow. Oh, how much did I ever miss them, and how much I cared for them. But I did not even know if they were okay out there in this very destructive weather.

It had been twenty-four hours since I last saw them, since I last spoke with them. It happened so fast from the moment I jumped off my boat into the water, and minutes later I was on the fisherman's motorboat and then taken away to the village and accommodated by the hospitality of the village chief and his loving, caring family. Every hour seemed like an eternity! I thought, *How much longer before the weather gets better? How many more days will I have to wait in anxiety, not knowing anything about their safety?* My imagination had now gotten a hold of me and was driving me crazy.

The next morning, even before dawn, the village chief and the commander of the naval base told me that there would be a break for about five to six hours before the weather got ugly again. He said that we all should take advantage of this break in the weather to start looking for my people. This news came to me at no better a time, for I would have gone insane if I had to just sit in the house and wait longer. I was so very happy. The weather got a lot better overnight, and despite what the forecast said, I prayed that this storm would come to an end soon so that normal life could resume in this village and elsewhere, and for me, that I was able to find my family and my companions.

The commander turned to me and said, "Here is a pair of binoculars, a map, and my patrol boat. You go with my trooper to find your people, and make it quick before it gets worse. Good luck on your mission."

I then said thank you to both the chief and the commander for their loving kindness, especially to the chief and his family for taking good care of me the past few days.

This was a new day as the sun began to emerge at the horizon with such a beautiful pinkish color. The wind had completely subsided, allowing normal life to return to this small, remote village. It was called Liminangcong of Palawan of the Philippines. In the air birds had returned from their hiding places to sing their songs, greeting the new day, and on the ground, chickens and ducks were out feeding. Here and there a few dogs and puppies were out playing. The air of this morning felt so fresh, and the breeze brought the aroma of the after-rain fragrance, the pleasant but almost indescribable mixture of wet soil, grass, leaves, dew, and who knows what other ingredients of nature. I was very upbeat and in high spirits and anxious to follow the military serviceman, a sergeant, to be exact, of the Philippine navy to the dock where the patrol boat was waiting for us. This was the very same dock to which the fisherman had brought me so that I could feel the solid soil under my feet after so many days on the dangerous water. It was dark and under the downpour of the rainstorm. If I had not been in such physical and emotional distress, I would have otherwise felt that I had been saved and was safe.

Before the boat took off from its mooring post, I showed the sergeant the area on the map where we had lost and been separated from the other boat at the beginning of the storm a few days ago. He said he had been briefed about the situation and was very familiar with the area. He was in very high spirits as well and had a sense of determination to accomplish his mission, which was to find my people and to bring them safely home. I felt so very good about him, about his aura, about his sense of confidence, and perhaps, most of all, his profound enthusiasm. Now the boat was on its way, cutting the colorful surface of the water, which reflected the morning sun from the horizon. The sound of the engine and the waves, the wake with clear transparent bubbles left behind the boat, and the breeze from the sea caressed my face and my neck, bringing chills to my body. All this heightened my spirits and my hopes. After weaving and curving and passing by a few islands, we were approaching the area of water where we had been lost in our separation. We looked to the left of us. The sand beach stretched for less than a mile, lying peacefully next to the quiet, motionless water. There was no wreckage or debris from the boat, nor was there anything that could indicate any misfortunes of my circumstance. I looked harder beyond the line of sand into the bushes, the trees, to find anything that was moving, anything that would give signs to me that my people were alive in this quiet, beautiful morning. The sun was rising up higher at the horizon, and it dawned on me that I had not seen the sun for many days. It did bring warmth and hope and energized me after many gloomy cold days.

A few birds were stretching their wings on the air as if they were racing against my boat, which was now almost leaving the beach behind. My thinking now went back to moments of losing sight of my boat three days ago in this very vicinity. If the boat was lost to the wind that evening and if the boat captain lost control of his boat and if the boat had capsized right here, then where was it, where were my companions, my wife, and my children? Instead of being disappointed at the fact that they were nowhere to be found around here in this area, I felt the sense of their being alive and safe and that they were somewhere not too far from here. I looked at the sergeant, and as if reading my thoughts, reading my mind and agreeing to it, he gave me a little smile, a wink, and a nod of assurance and of encouragement all in one as he was standing maneuvering the boat, helping me looking for my people, my family. As the boat was moving along the shoreline in the same channel of the water, I began to use the binoculars, through which I was able to look farther to the left of me, where there was another island. I could see nothing but trees and rocks along the edge of the water. I moved my search to the right of me. The lenses of this gadget were able to capture the scenery ahead of me in detail. Along the waterline, sea lions were on their food hunt up and down from the surface of the water, and the birds were also in competition for their fish as well, but nothing turned up as we continued our search.

We were anxious but in no rush to move along the water lines. I found that the green trees and forest accented with some light amber to orange colors of the leaves along the edge of the water were so naturally beautiful, and we wanted to make sure we did not miss anything. There were some giant rocks or boulders butted together, creating a cave-like space, but no one was in there. Perhaps this was a nesting place for the sea lions to come stay after a hardworking day. *Where are they hiding?* I wondered as a thought more than a question that just popped up in my head. Could they have been pushed back into the sea that night? We had used up the last can of fuel, and therefore, the engine might not have enough of it to keep the boat moving. If it were the case, then it was at the mercy of the wind and the rain that night, and

God knew what might have happened. I definitely needed to get myself off from this kind of thinking and keep myself focused on looking and watching.

We continued on course, heading to the last two islands before getting out into the sea where we came in three days ago. The sun was up a little higher at my left, making the water in front of me blue and so beautiful. Fish were at their morning play here and there up in the air. They swooped down back into the clear water and up again as they were having the fun of their time. I adjusted the lenses of my binoculars, and I could pick up some objects far away. Oh yes, I had just spotted a white object moving back and forth as some sort of a signal for us. My heart was pounding faster than the speed of this boat because I knew instinctively in my heart that it was a signal from my people, but I doubted that they knew it was I who was coming to their rescue. I immediately let the sergeant know that I had found them and pointed my finger in their direction. With a big smile on his dark-skinned face, as if sharing my excitement, my happiness, he gave me a thumbs-up and threw both of his arms into the air in the state of ecstasy of joy.

As the boat picked up its speed, so did the wind against my face, as if to make sure that I was fully awake for the next moments of excitement, the moments of the reunion of my family. I could see my people gathering at the shoreline next to a hut, waving their hands toward me, and the boat, their boat, I mean, was there as well, but not next to them. It was somehow tucked under the canopy of a tree not too far from where they were standing. Yes, it was our boat. The light green color with red stripes at the front and the shape of the canopy in the back covering the engine compartment gave its identity, and yes, it was my people who were now waving faster for help as if we would pass them by and miss them. I could see them now very clearly. Men and women and children were all out in the clear, beautiful sunshine, all in their excitement waving and waving and screaming as if to make sure they got our attention. But the question in my curious mind was that how in heaven had the boat gotten to the spot where it was now. It was as if someone had picked the toy boat up and set it right there underneath the tree. And my God, it was not. It was at least a couple thousand pounds in weight. It must have been some sort of miracle to have it happen. I hoped someone would tell me what had happened and how it got there.

The sergeant slowed his patrol boat down when we were about hundred yards away from the beach; my poor people were all lined up along the waterline. Everyone waved at me and gave me their beautiful smiles, and I gave mine to them with a silent apology that I had abandoned them for the last three days, especially to my wife and my children. As the engine became quiet and the boat pushed aground, I got off the boat onto the sand and embraced my children with tears of joy in this spectacular reunion of my family. This was the happiest day of my life, as I had lost my family and now had found them again. Of course, they were very happy to see me again. They must have had their hearts break for not knowing what happened to me that very evening or where I was taken to when that wall of rain and wind separated us. Now that everyone was out from the boat, they were all out on the ground and were as happy as they could be, for they knew that they were now safe and that they were going to be taken to the US or Philippine bases from where they would be accepted and resettled in the United States or other countries of their dreams. I now saw many faces I had never before seen. That was the very reason the boat was overpacked and laden heavily to the sinking point. The boat owner had concerns over the possibility that someone in our core group had received some sort of payment, be it in gold, diamonds, or even cash, to let them on board. I would soon find out, and I would make this matter transparent to everyone involved so that all misunderstandings among us could be cleared up.

Everyone was now talking, telling stories—the stories of their lives, the story that would forever change not only their own lives, but the lives of their children and grandchildren as well. They relived their emotions, their anxieties, their uncertainties, and the dangers they had endured on their thousand-mile journey to the Philippines. They were now all relaxed and waiting to be boarded on this patrol boat.

The boat captain deserved all the credit, for he made the quick turn of his boat and went with the wind the moment of our separation, the minute that the center of the typhoon and storm hit us. He did exactly what I had hoped and anticipated in order to survive the wrath of Mother Nature. Lots of water had flooded into the boat, and they were all busy, bucket after bucket, emptying it out back into the sea. As the boat survived the quick shock of a turn, the rain kept pouring down; the captain could barely see where he was heading his boat. The wind and the rain combined beating on his boat, so he had no choice but to let the wind do the pushing; and at the same time, he veered his boat to the right as his instinct guided him, and finally he reached the beach of this island.

Just before this happened, the propeller of his boat hit an unknown object, be it coral rock or a piece of drifting wood, and became useless. Fortunately, the tide was quite high and the strong wind helped push the boat aground to where it was under the tree. I could not help but think how lucky, how fortunate we all were. If the propeller had been broken farther out from this shoreline, the boat could have drifted away and capsized, and we would never ever have found them. We had so much to be thankful for.

As these survivors were telling the story. I recognized they were all miracles, one after another. When the boat was aground at this very beach, there was a hut built by and for the farmers who lived on this island. My people fought the rain and the wind, seeking shelter inside the hut, and that very night, a baby was born, a boy, making him the second angel born on our trip. I remembered the mother of this baby whom I saw and met at the village at the time we were making arrangements to hide our people in each of the houses in the village. She was a daughter of the household who said that she would like to come along. Looking at the size of her baby inside her, I asked when she was due.

"I will have my baby in a few days, Uncle." She addressed me as her uncle because of my age, not because of family ties. I thought she was just joking and that she had no intention to be on our boat, risking her life and the life of her baby. She then disappeared into the house, and I went on my business, making sure things were going exactly as planned. Now she was right here, very happy with her tiny baby son among many other happy faces. I have to give her lots of credit for being so brave, or so desperate to get out of the country, without considering her own risk and that of her unborn child. I could now see on the faces of these people, young and old, the will, the determination to get on that boat even they knew the chance of survival was less than 50 percent. They just wanted the freedom to grow as human beings, as they all deserved. I could see in these people of mine the infinite potentiality to grow, and their future was lying ahead, waiting for them. Oh yes, I, among all of them, could feel the miracle that brought us here unharmed, despite the turmoil of the sea and especially the turbulence of the weather of the past days. I also recognized the bond that held us together during our journey, be it in our prayers or in our sharing of our concerns, our worries, and encouragement.

I felt the invisible hands of the divine lift and guide our boat through the dangers and our plight on the high seas. This was the moment of reunion for all of us, the moment that brought us to the realization that we were now safe and that we should be celebrating this very moment with joy and gratefulness. There was another tale being told about the touch of divine on my people during the first hours of their arrival. Once they were inside the hut, where it was warmer and safer for them, even though they could hardly move about because the floor space was limited and they were large in number, danger was lurking outside. While the wind was beating on the side of the hut, howling, shaking, and threatening to blow it off the ground, at the same time, the rain was doing its very best to beat down the hut. Meanwhile, on the hillside, a large boulder rolled down the hill, only missing the outside of the hut by a couple of meters, eventually coming to rest at the edge of the water. To me, it was not luck; it was definitely an act of the saving grace from the divine that touched upon us from the very beginning of our journey. I would not want to imagine what could have happened if the boulder rolled right through inside of the hut. The mood of our reunion would have been the opposite; instead, it would be that of a funeral. It was another blessing to be acknowledged among many others.

The sun was high casting its warm rays on all of us; the breeze was bringing freshness of the sea as if saying, "Rejuvenate my people, for you all deserve the goodness of this nature."

The green leaves of the tress, especially the branches on the high trunks of the coconut palm trees, were all waving as if they were dancing with us in this moment of joy as we began embarking on the rescue boat, one by one, children with their moms to be helped on board first, and then men last, with very few to none of the belongings. We bade farewell to the villagers who had extended their kindness in letting us into their hut. They also were angels of the heaven who helped my people in their distressed hours of their arrival at this beach and allowed them not only a stay in their hut but also shared with them food, which was not ample on this island. How could one repay the kindness one received? It is almost impossible! For these simple, kind-hearted, but not well-to-do folks in this village, it would not be realistic to say that someday we would return here to pay them a visit or to pay them back for what they gave us, even though in our hearts, we wanted someday to do just that. But in our situation, as refugees, we had no clue where we were or where we were going or how far it was from here. The only one thing we knew for sure was we were now safe from the storm, from hunger, and we owed it to their kindness. They did it out of their hearts. They did it out of their kindness and never expected any return. Blessed are their hearts! It is the law of nature, the law of hearts! I would like to call it the law of kindness in which one can almost return the kindness one received by extending it to everyone, everywhere and everytime.

The radio transmissions in the language of Tagalog, intermixed with English, spoken between the sergeant and his command, was now at its peak. The local indigenous voice sounded like continuous notes of fast-moving high-toned music that fit perfectly into this situation. I had not had a chance to hear the sound from the use of this gadget since the end of the war. That was almost five years ago. The on and off, the stop and go of each transmission brought me a very good and happy feeling, the feeling of being connected to the world, the feeling of being in communication with the person at the other end. And in this case, it gave me a feeling of being alive in every possible sense. The joyful mood of everyone on this boat was such a relief for me. Everyone knew that they were being transported to the military base in the Philippines, where they were going to be, later on, shipped to the refugee camp located in the Western Command. I was asked by the sergeant to relay this message to everyone on board.

The load on this boat was now quite heavy as opposed to what it was a few hours ago. Every inch of space on this boat was filled with my people, many of whom I had never met before. Some of us adult men were to stand to give spaces to others. The boat now was heading back to its base at the same speed as it took off at this morning. It was in a careful motion earlier to make sure that we would not miss anything in the searching for them, and now it was to be sure to bring us home safe and sound. The sun was now high, and the sky was cloudless blue. The stretch of the water ahead of us was flat and peaceful. The islands on my right and the beach on my left were all at peace after the angry storm. We were all being absorbed in this very moment of peacefulness of life as the boat continued its course to its home base. The happy faces of my people, caressed by the breeze, with their eyes fixed on the scenery, seemed to be taking in all the beauty of the nature and having the sense of wonder from the many twists of life. I just wondered if any one of these folks would have anything in their mind and their hearts other than a sense of awe and gratefulness. I doubted it.

At last, far ahead of us appeared houses among the coconut trees with a few limbs hanging loosely at the sides of their trunks.

A couple of battle ships of the Philippine Navy showing their weaponry with tall watchtowers were anchored at their hub off the shoreline. As we came closer to the base, we noticed that these ships were in their mode to receive us. The soldiers were off on the deck, waving to us with their hands and smiles on their faces. They shared with us the joy of being lost and then found; they shared with us the pride of their mission accomplished in searching and rescuing us. They were there to save our lives; they were out there to rescue those in distress, in danger, regardless of the political mood of their government, which, at that time, regarded the early comers of the boat people as "illegal entries."

I did also notice, to my very surprise and awe, that my boat was moored not too far from another ship. It meant that my brother-in-law had arrived here safely because he was on that very boat when it took off from Cam Ranh Bay earlier. We had been waiting for news of his arrival, but it had not come prior to our escape. This was my very first boat that I had built after the village chief endorsed my petition to get my old boat enlarged. I could not get away with it because all people in the village knew that I was going to escape with it, so I had to change my plan of action. One idea was to divert people's attention on me. I secretly sold my boat to people from another village with the condition that my brother-in-law, Thi, could come along free of charge. The night it took off to the high seas was the night I stopped by to visit and to say good-bye to Thi, who was already on the boat. I then walked away. Those who watched me would know that I was not on the boat, and therefore, they did not pay any attention to it. As a result, it took off at midnight without any difficulties. Now that I knew he was there, I was anxious to join him soon.

As our boat slowed, I wondered where it would stop—at a pier at the village, or by the battle ships? But it did not take very long to see that it was headed to the side of its mother ship, where the sergeant killed the engine and instructed us to stay put until they cleared all procedures of getting us on to the big ship.

A small rope was used as a tool to get a good head count. It was stretched about a foot off the top of the front deck of the boat, and everyone who crossed the rope was helped by the hands of the navy men onto the ship and was counted. It began with the mothers, their infants and other children, and then finally, the rest of us men who all crossed the line and were accounted for.

The crossing of this line brought me a sudden realization of the importance of this point in my life. Crossing this rope brought me into the world of the unknown, but one full of possibilities of safety and happiness. But, at the same time, it separated me from my future and my past. I chose to leave behind the shadows of the old days, the days of torture, imprisonment, and sadness, the days of hunger and injustice. This was the moment of my enlightenment.

Was I ready for the head count after everyone was accounted for? The process was not complicated and was done in less than an hour with the help of two officers and their assistants. With two clipboards and marking pens, every person who crossed the line onto the deck of the ship was recorded with his name and date of birth. This information was then reported to the government of the Philippines as well as to the United Nations High Commissioners for Refugees (UNHCR). We were at the number of 105 bodies and souls, which included the two newborn babies who decided to join us during our journey. How amazing! What a miracle! A tiny boat on which we initially planned to have a maximum of thirty people, all of whom were our family members, who contributed time and materials and finances and effort to make it happen, now turned out to be almost quadrupled. The boat made it there in spite of the typhoon and the storm. Not only did it not lose anyone, but it gained two new people to this wonderful world. It must have been the work of the divine indeed.

It was late in the evening after the commander congratulated me and the rest of my group of people on our safe arrival. He then informed me that a military chaplain was going to be flown in and a Thanksgiving mass would be held right on the ship.

A middle-aged Catholic chaplain, a captain in his military uniform, arrived shortly after that on his helicopter from the

Western Command. He was greeted warmly by his navy crew on the ships and of course, by all of us as well. He had been briefed on our situation and circumstances and genuinely shared his joy on our safe arrival. He said that divine intervention had definitely touched everyone of us during our journey and that we should celebrate and give thanks to the Lord, to the God who showed his mercy and saved us all. A table was quickly brought to the cabin of the ship, and a white tablecloth was placed on top of it, and voila, it became an altar. The priest now put on his festive religious robes, and the shiny gold cups, water bottles, and the hosts were now placed on the altar. The mass was about to begin. This small but fully attentive and grateful congregation from all different religious beliefs, be it Buddhism, Catholicism, ancestor worshippers, or other faiths, was now gathered in a semicircle in front of the altar. The priest walked to the front of the altar and faced all of us. He looked at each of us in the eye, and in this brief moment of silence, we deepened the connectedness between us and the spirit of God. His opening prayer was that he welcomed all of us here, and he reminded us that God had extended his hands to save us through the storm, through the weather, and that as good, faithful people, we needed to be thankful to him. The priest also asked us to have our full attention and meditation on this theme of being grateful and thankful. I was asked to serve as altar boy. I conducted the readings and translated his brief sermon on the readings. The air of this service was one of absolute solemnity and was filled with spirit of the divine. It was an interesting notion of enlightenment for me in this moment that we all came from different backgrounds, different religious faiths with all different beliefs, but we knelt down and bowed our heads to one God.

I remember the famous saying of an Indian saint, Mahatma Gandhi, who said, "In heaven there are no religions." And in this moment full of spirit, I acknowledged that the spirit of God was in each one of us. This alone brought tears to my eyes.

Outside, the sunlight faded away. The rain began to pour down on the ship. The weather seemed to cooperate very well with us, as it gave my people just enough time to get safely to the ship. I expressed my appreciation and gratitude to the chaplain on behalf of my group, a group of 105, now known to the representatives of the United Nations and to the Philippine government as well. I subsequently saw this priest many times at the refugee camp in Palawan since he was the only chaplain for the Western Command at that time.

After the spiritual service, we were asked to join the ship captain, his wife, and other staff and crew in the mess hall for dinner. I was asked to tell the story of our escape that began ten days earlier. All the memories came back to me as fresh as yesterday, and I retold the stories with all of my emotion and conviction in all the details in executing our plan of escape. My story won the sympathy of my new audience, especially the commander and his wife. Our leadership group of men, the boat captain, his assistant, and a few other friends of mine were given special treatment by the commander. We were offered separate living quarters with bunk beds, and the rest of our group stayed in other parts of the ship. I felt a bit uncomfortable at this arrangement. I would rather be together with my family, for we had been separated for a very long time. But after all, we were guests of the commander and his ship. I thought I'd better be happy with whatever was given, and I shouldn't have asked for more.

The commander was in his later forties and showed a special interest and respect toward me as he asked me about my past service and if I had been in the United States. I told him where I hoped to be was the US and that it would be my very first time to be on US soil. My past association with America was to have served with the US Special Forces. I told him of the many operations, the many patrols that I had participated in while in the DBT USSF training center. I even told him episodes of my tour of duty at A-232 Special Forces camp, which was under mortar and artillery attack, and that I had survived. I told him of my then commander, Captain Raymond Striler, who, weeks later, decided to ship me out of the camp on a helicopter for fear that I was too young to get killed. Shortly after my new assignment to the B23rd Headquarters, which was located in the heart of the city of Ban Me Thuot, I was informed that my new replacement had been shot in the head by a bullet from a sniper outside the camp. I felt forever indebted to Captain Striler, who saved my life. I also told the commander that I hoped someday when I was in the US, I would find Captain Striler to have the honor to tell him how grateful I was to him for his decision to transfer me out of the war zone, which saved my life. I would never know the motive behind his decision to get me out, but I deeply appreciated his actions.

As the dinner was winding down, we were excused to our living quarters. My companion, a former officer, a major in the VN armed forces, told me how much he appreciated my making the connection with the commander of this ship and his staff and his crew. He was thankful for the special treatment that was given to all of us, which seemed to be a result of my diplomacy. I felt a little elated, for this was the first time someone in my group as a companion, as a friend, had shown an appreciation toward my efforts. His name was Mr. Luong. He later helped me tremendously in running the refugee camp. There were other issues among us that needed to be resolved, one of which was the charge from the boat owner and the boat captain who had thought that I might have accepted monies or fees in gold from some of the uninvited guests that were among us on this ship. However, we were all very tired, and I did not want to pursue the issue at this point in time. We needed some rest first, and I would have to deal with this in the next few days or so to clear me out of this mud of misunderstanding. It was the best sleeping night I had for a very long time, perhaps in weeks. I must have slept like a stone, for when I woke up to the noise and commotions from my companions, it was time for breakfast.

What? Breakfast served on the ship to us? It was hard to believe, but it was a reality. We were treated very kindly; the comradeship among us was always shown. The sailors here on the water and us, the former foot-fighters, had something in common, and we could feel the connectedness. The showers on the ship made me feel fortunate and privileged, as did the breakfast and dinner we were served. I also discovered that the Filipino diet was very much the same as ours. Fish and rice were our main courses in every meal; that is why we did not miss our food very much during our stay on the ship. Canned fish, dried fish, and fresh fish soup together with rice kept us filled and happy every day. The commander and his wife were with us every day, especially in the evening. He talked about his military life and his family far away in Manila and how much he had missed them. Now that his wife, to whom he had been married for a year, was with him all the time, he felt less lonesome. He asked me to tell my people that he would offer highest US dollars for gold from Vietnam, which was twenty-four-karat gold. My family and I were penniless. We had no gold or silver. Mr. Ngoi, the boat captain, who, through the rumors, carried a sandbag full of gold, did make some sale of his precious metal for the greenbacks and subsequently shopped at the local store in the village for necessities. My wife also sold our only wedding ring for pesos to buy two pairs of slippers for our sons. That was only thing we could afford for our kids.

A final notice from the commander that we would be transferred by ship to the refugee camp in Palawan in twenty-four hours shortened our days on the ships. The news brought us mixed emotions. We would be glad and happy to be in the refugee camp, where we would be screened and interviewed for different resettlement programs. But at the same time, we would miss these soldiers whom we had come to know and felt attached to through their kindness. For me, I felt deeply attached to not only these sailors, but also to the village chief and his family, who had taken care of me from the first night of my arrival under the storm. I certainly prayed and hoped deeply in my heart that their good-heartedness would be rewarded abundantly. I was also deeply saddened to say good-bye to all of them, and I told them that I would treasure them in my heart for all the goodness they had given me. I hoped some day I would see them again.

We boarded the cargo ship the next day en route to the refugee camp. It would take several hours to get there, but it did not bother us a bit. This was a ship four times the size of our boat, equipped with all modern gadgetry and ready for all kinds of weather. Besides, it traveled at a speed and distance that we could still enjoy the landscape of this part of the Philippines.

The weather was fair, with some clouds hanging over our heads; it was just a beautiful morning to be on the water. The seagulls were gliding on their wings, making their morning cries over the sky, and the fish were doing their show along the ship. The aroma of the salt air added to make a complete panorama of beauty and bliss. It was quite a lively atmosphere. As I was in this meditative moment, taking in the wonders of the nature while I was standing at the front deck, a navy uniformed officer, whom I had not seen in the last few days, came over to introduce himself. He was a petty officer of the ship, and we started our conversation. He told me about his military life, ten years in the service, a family of a wife and a daughter living in a village somewhere near Manila. I told him about mine and that I was going to the United States of America. He said he wished that he were in my situation. There was a quiet moment between our conversations; then I was a bit startled at the notion of his wishing. Here he was, an officer in his early forties; the future in his own control, I assumed; the top rung of his military ladder was there for him to attain, yet he wished to exchange his status for mine, the one of an "illegal entry." We would not earn the title of being a refugee until officially registered with the UNHCR. I asked him why he said what he had said.

"Well," he said in his monotone voice with lightly accented English, "all you have to do is to escape, to cross the sea, and you have a chance to come to America, and I, unless I have a lot of money, which I don't, would never be able to be there to live. America is a dream of the many of us Filipinos, and for the rest of my life, I don't think I can make it there."

I felt the air was a bit heavy between us; I was trying to make some sense out of what he was saying. Was it a self-assessing of his dilemma? Or was it an expression of jealousy in disguise? Did he know what we had been through? I wished that I could tell him the stories of the pregnant moms delivering their babies on the boat, delivering their babies in the hut at the shoreline of an island. It was a risky business trying to make the escape. It was so risky that not many were willing to try. Would he do it if he knew that he had only less than half of a chance of survival? Would he do it if he knew that the chances were good that he would become food for the sharks in the sea? But we did it for the sake of freedom, for the sake of having opportunities to live and do and be what we possibly could be. I wished I could tell him that, but instead I kept silent. I kept my status as well as my thoughts to myself. I did not want to make him upset, or, as old saying goes, "rock the boat."

Nothing much really had happened during our transit except we had more canned mackerel for our meals, and I felt that I would not be able to handle canned fish for the rest of my life. But as always, I am forever grateful, for I got my fill.

PUERTO PRINCESSA

Upon our arrival in the city Puerto Princessa, we were loaded on a truck headed to the refugee camp. We felt that it was a long time we were on the truck even though it was only a few miles away. I was very anxious to see what a refugee camp looked like. How many people were there in the camp? How was the life over there? What kind activities were there, and so on and so forth. Question after question just heightened my curiosity and my anxiousness, and our arrival seemed never to come.

At last, the truck went through the gate after the driver had checked in with the rifled guards. We unloaded ourselves with our little belongings next to the shade of a sizable tamarind tree. We were immediately surrounded with tons of those who had come earlier. They were very happy to see us. They were talking, pointing their fingers as if trying to identify their relatives and acquaintances. All of this, together with the sounds and the noise from the loudspeakers announcing our arrival, made this seem like a rowdy party. My wife and I and our boys spotted Thi coming over, and we waved to each other happily. We told him that we had seen his boat and expected to see him. We were then advised to come and stay inside the office for registration, and when finished, we would be assigned to living quarters in the camp, at which time we could see and talk all we wanted to anyone we wanted.

"Group 105" became the legal identity of our group for the management of the camp and the Western Command. I made my first observations about the camp from this spot. It was located right off the beach, sort of a rocky one, flanked with lots of tall coconut trees from the south side and an airfield from the north for military landings and takeoffs. The whole camp was bordered with barbed wire and was strictly patrolled by armed military personnel. The camp dwellings were built with thatched roofs, or to be exact, with coconut palm leaves and split bamboo walls. The communal ones were rather large. The one almost across from the main office was an example. It was about four thousand square feet with bamboo bunk beds stacked up to three levels, almost up to the roof. Besides the communal ones, there were single-unit huts owned by individuals as well. From the office I could almost see the whole camp because the building was partially walled—just the roof and the bamboo poles to support it—and it was centrally located. The camp area was roughly four acres of land divided into four zones for management purposes.

Mr. Quy Vinh Le, the chairman and director of the camp, a former attorney, along with Mr. Thanh Vuong Dinh, a former police officer and karate instructor, came to introduce themselves to us. From what I observed and was told by the management team, all volunteers from the community of displaced people like me and others present here were to work to improve the life of individual boat people and to make the camp as a whole a nice and warm place to live. General Fernandez, commanding officer of the Western Command, assigned a military officer, Lt.Pagaduan, to work with the camp director and his management team. He had three NCOs and guards to ensure their military presence at the camp.

I looked up at the operations chart on the wall. In the arrivals column, my group was just now chalked up, group 105, bringing the total of refugees over two thousand. I also noticed that there were a few lines of numbers on the departure column. It gave me a sense of balancing the incomings and outgoings of the population of the camp. However, at this rate, the camp would explode with more coming in and fewer going out.

There were two long, wooden tables and benches on the dirt floor. The volunteers were doing an excellent job getting us registered as quickly as they could with what they had. Pens and paper were used to record names, dates of birth, and the whole personal history of each person. It was so important, so vital, that the information provided and recorded must be absolutely correct because it was going to be registered or shared with many different agencies. The most important was the UNHCR, the United Nations, and the Western Military Command. The UNHCR would then feed the information and data to different embassies for their selection of candidate refugees for their programs. Those refugees who fit into their criteria would be screened, interviewed, and finally approved, and then the happy moment would come, to be airlifted to undergo medical processing in Manila then to be sent to the final destination. This sounded simple, but in reality, it was not, as I later discovered. The information provided sometimes got exaggerated or condensed, or sometimes even fabricated to fit into their situation or their desires.

When the registration for my family was completed, we were then assigned to a building in zone four, where some of people in my group were also staying. We all were happy together again. Thi also moved in with us, leaving behind his short-lived life with his single friends whom he had met at his arrival at the camp. We were extremely happy to have found him here, and we were able to get him to join together with us under one roof. He told us that he had contacted our cousins who had come to the United States at the time of the fall of the Saigon government in 1975. He and his family were among the many lucky ones who had made it to the US Navy ships that were out in the international waters to pick up refugees.

Zone four was located at the end of the airstrip; in fact, all of the camp was at the end of the airfield, and it was so close that sometimes we felt we could touch the landing aircrafts approaching from our end or from the sea. Our location had one advantage over the rest of the camp; that is, at the end of our zone was a huge drainpipe bringing rainwater from the runway. We often came to this spot because of its cement platform that flared out at the end of the pipe, which gave us plenty of room for a bath or for washing our clothes. At this point in time, drinking water was brought in from outside the camp. A military vehicle hauled it in every morning, and a tanker of water was left at the yard in front of the office for distribution. Water was rationed according to the size of the family; we were given enough for cooking only. Washing and bathing were done at the communal waterpump. This well was dug with a metal pipe driven into the ground where there were lots of lava rocks and boulders. I just wondered if there was anyone who questioned the intelligence of picking out this very location for a water supply, but as time went on, I discovered that the whole camp was set on an area that had many rocks in the ground. Therefore, it would not matter where the well was dug. The water was only good for washing. It did have a little taste of being salty, not as strong as that of the sea, but you got a sticky feeling after a bath. Because of this, fresh water became a hot commodity, not for sale, but for preservation.

It did not take me very long to get involved in the activities of helping the camp management. In fact, after a few days of getting some rest, I volunteered to help by having two English classes, one in the morning and the other in the afternoon, all of which were free, and all were welcome. Besides these public classes, I was often requested to teach private lessons for individuals during my spare time for a fee. Not long after my involvement in teaching, there was a request from a gentleman who suggested that he would organize a class in the evening for adults only. He would also be responsible for classroom space as well as collecting small fees from each student. All I had to do was show up to teach for one hour, and the rest was his. I was beginning to be busy and getting busier, as I was voted to become a zone leader of zone four. As such, I was also a member of camp council, a voting body that selected the chairman of the camp. I was also asked to sit in on many screening interviews by delegations from various embassies to select candidate refugees for their resettlement programs.

One interviewing session I found both a little amusing and educational. I sat in as an interpreter for a US delegation. Mary and Tom, the interviewers from the J.V.A (Joint Voluntary Agency), a part of the US embassy in the Philippines, must have done lots of interviews and had a keen awareness and sensitivity to the falseness and the truth of statements made by refugees. They seemed to know whether the information given was somewhat fabricated or totally untrue.

There was a young couple who had been in the camp for almost five months who also claimed to have been married for more than a year, months before their escape from Vietnam. They were asked to give all personal information such as date of birth, place of birth, place of schooling, name of parents, place of residence, and finally, date and place of their wedding. All this seemed to match what was individually declared upon their arrival at the camp. It was "so far so good" as one might say. But suddenly, Tom focused on the guy as he intensified his questioning. Tom's thinking was that if this young couple was truly married prior to their escape, then they would have surely known about their dwelling and their environment. They should be able to answer a few simple questions about their house. The wife was asked to sit way back by the wall, where she would not be able to hear what was being asked of her husband. Tom then asked him if he remembered there was a well at his house. His answer was yes. The next question concerned the location of the well in relation to the house. The young man said without any hesitation that it was located in front but more to the right of the house. Was there a fruit tree of any kind right next to it? He said a papaya tree was there when he left.

Now came his wife's turn as Tom asked her husband to stay far back from the table where we were sitting. All the same questions were directed to her, but she was not sure, and she said she had forgotten all these details. The interviewers, Tom and Mary, somehow had discerned the fabrication of their marriage while in the camp. They told me that the young man, according to the information received, was initially qualified for the US program.

Because he now falsely claimed to be married to a lady whom he recently met at the camp, both of them were disqualified for the US program, but they might be able to apply for other countries. I felt sorry for this couple, and at the same time, I was amazed at what was going on at the refugee camp where things were manipulated or fabricated for one's own interest. I would have never thought of the questions Tom and Mary used to bring about the truth when they did the interviews. I was also amused at the questions they had at the other interviews in which they asked the applicant if he or she knew the colors of the ceiling of their bedroom back in Vietnam if they claimed to be a wedded couple. I teased them that out of the two of them, the only one who would know was the wife. They gave me a dirty look after a moment to get the meaning of my comment.

Things were going well for me at the camp, as I fully engaged into all kinds of activities of the camp. Mr. Thanh, the head of the internal security team, which was a part of the management, came to me with a report of incidents in which the Filipino military personnel had beaten the refugees. This report was in Vietnamese, detailing the beating using rifle butts on the refugees who at the time were regarded as illegal entries. What Thanh wanted me to do was have this report translated into English so that it could be sent to churches and charitable organizations as well as to the UNHCR to make them all aware of the conditions of the refugees at the camp. I saw the benefits and the impact the report would have made on the lives of refugees in this camp. Therefore I jumped right into it as he had wished without giving any thought that I could get myself in a lot of trouble with the Western Command if they knew I was the one who did the report. Nevertheless, I finished it and handed it to him as soon as it was done.

There was a young pastor—we called him Pastor Vidal—a young Filipino man, who would come to see us, Group 105, at our living quarters to talk about his church and to ask us to go to church with him on Sundays. One day he brought in some clothes and shoes for the people in my group to use. A few days after that, he brought in some cups of noodles, which I knew were not enough to give to everyone in the group. I then decided to let some of the people in the group living in my quarters have them. The result was that I got blamed for not sharing with other people of my group who stayed in other areas. This went to the management, and I had to do a lot of explaining and defending myself for what I did. I guess I was prone to being blamed, even from the beginning of my journey on the sea. I finally cleared myself from this little mess, but those who wanted to get me into the mud were not happy, for I was still on my feet and fully engaging in working and serving the camp. A person who was sore on this whole thing was a former captain of military police, who was in charge of legal team. He failed to prove that I was guilty, and as result, he was never friendly with me.

As a representative of zone four, I was in every council meeting and other meeting where the military officers from the Western Command were present to discuss the ways to improve the life of the refugees. I always engaged myself wholeheartedly in the discussion and conversations with the uniformed officers to get my point across, and as a result, I gradually gained the respect from my colleagues and the military command as well. Life at the camp improved tremendously; more people were brought in from the sea, and more were leaving the camp for a better life somewhere in another country.

Branches of services at the camp such as education, social services, and medical care were the ones doing notably well thanks to the volunteerism among the refugees themselves and from the local Red Cross chapter in Puerto Princessa city and other charitable agencies.

I found a new friend who was in charge of medical care, Dr. Timothy Vo, or Dr. Thanh, his Vietnamese name. Thanh had arrived at the camp in the early stages of the formation of this facility. He was a rather young man in his late twenties, a dedicated physician, and a refugee who graduated from medical school in Saigon a few years before the fall of Saigon government. His trip to this land from Vietnam was quite sorrowful and eventful.

He almost lost his life to the sea when his boat ran into low-tide coral and got stuck for days. They ran out of food and water, and many of his companions had decided to leave the boat, swimming away and disappearing into the vastness of the sea. Some of those who stayed gradually died of hunger and thirst. He was one of very few survivors when his boat came to float as high tide returned. Dr. Vo brought with him not only the knowledge of his field of medicine, but also a rare dedication that won the respect of all in the camp and the military personnel as well. He was a letterman as well as an artist himself. His painting and writing and calligraphy were very impressive. Later in our friendship, I discovered that he was a seminarian who had longed to become a priest in the Catholic Church but decided against it. His office and clinic was also where he stayed. The four hundred-square-foot space upstairs was where he conducted his business and saw his refugee patients.

My stay at the camp entered into the third month. With teaching and being fully engaged in many activities of the camp, I felt a bit overwhelmed but enjoyed the time and the service. Then came time for the election to elect the director of the camp, which had been a tradition here. Every three months, the council would have a vote to elect a new leader, a chairman for the camp.

The morning of the election came. All the council members were present at the office to cast their votes. The mood of the camp was on the solemn side, and the air in the office was filled with seriousness of the matter. It did not matter who would be the next chairman as long as he could work along with the military officers and was willing to compromise for the good and welfare of the refugees in the camp. I wanted to see the incumbent chairman, Mr. Quy Vinh Le, a former attorney in Saigon who was in his early fifties and who had been doing an excellent job as chairman, be reelected. I came to respect his maturity as well as his flair of diplomacy. With such admiration for him, I did cast my vote, thinking that all would have voted for him.

The reality, however, was very unexpected. I ended up getting their votes of confidence. I was utterly surprised, or to be exact, I was in total shock at the outcome. I had never thought of running for this position and never wanted it at all. To keep the military content and the refugee population of over 2,500 people happy was a job I would have never wanted. As the youngest person at the voting table now being elected, I truly wanted to decline the post. And therefore, I expressed this to the committee, for I felt that I had never in my life held any position of this nature and of importance.

But seeing all happy faces of these men who cheerfully congratulated me on the new post as their leader, I felt the call for service that was bestowed on me, and so I accepted the job as the third chairman of the camp. I thanked my colleagues for their votes of confidence and promised them the best of myself in serving the community of refugees here in Palawan, even though it was not my choice.

When the news got out, I was showered with congratulations from the military personnel, from the UNHCR, and from the churches. I knew immediately that the people who would be upset were my students, for I could no longer carry the load of teaching while running the camp. My very small income from private teaching and tutoring would have to come to an end. But one had to sacrifice sometimes for the good causes, and here was one of them for me.

As a weekly ritual of the camp, we would all gather on Mondays at the wide-open space area in front of the office for the Vietnamese flag ceremony in remembrance of the loved ones back home and those who lost their lives for the national causes.

At the Monday morning meeting after the election, I had to deliver a speech, an acceptance speech, to a large crowd of men and women and children. I must confess that I was so nervous and scared that I thought I would get stage fright. As the national anthem ended and the small yellow-orange flag with three red stripes, the Vietnamese national flag, was moving lively in the morning breeze on top of the flagpole, everyone was asked to be seated. The sun was rising high from the horizon, and the sky was blue and clear, promising a beautiful day. The council members, the camp management team members, and military personnel were seated in a row of folding chairs and benches facing the large crowd of refugees. I slowly rose from my chair, trying to keep my composure, and cast my eyes upon the crowd from end to end and on my colleagues. I delivered the very first public speech of my life at the age of thirty-two. I guess they all accepted me as their new chairman for the next three months, for I heard their loud hand clapping as they stood up. I thanked them for their trust in me, and in return, I asked them for their cooperation as I delivered my promise, my commitment to serving them.

The transfer of the chairmanship was nothing but a simple process. Mr. Quy Le was always helpful in guiding me to learn the ropes. I immediately had the support from Mrs. Schmidt, the commissioner for the United Nations for the Refugees (UNHCR). She knew that I had given up my income from teaching and was aware of everything else I had done up to that time. She also knew that what I was going to do was all based on volunteerism and dedication as a public servant, and as a result, she helped me with her own money, fifty dollars every month for four months until I left the camp. The JVA, Joint Voluntary Agency of the US Embassy in Manila, gave me their full support as well. I was well received by other delegations from the other embassies as time went on. My first round of diplomacy was in full swing.

I immediately intensified the working relationship with the military command, beginning with attaché officer, Lt. Pagaduane, and his NCOs, Sgt. Gomez and Sgt. Sabardo, all of whom were likable, and I did take advantage of this harmonious relationship. We strengthened and improved current programs and created new ones. The "green revolution" was widely received by the refugees, and it got full support from the military, the UN, and charitable organizations. It was a program in which everyone was encouraged to participate in growing their own vegetables for their own consumption. The first benefits from this program, as well as other programs, were first and foremost to keep all refugees from being idle, providing them with a positive attitude and the hope for their future. And the second one was physical fitness that would otherwise not be attained. In this program, the seeds of many kinds of vegetables such as mustard greens, Chinese greens, green beans, string beans, and squash of different kinds, were provided. To keep these greens growing, the military trucks hauled in tankers of fresh water for all to use, and the men and their veggies were all mutually happy.

The fishermen were now allowed to go fishing at night out in the sea, and their catches were sold back to the camp in the morning for cash. This fishing program was quite successful thanks to the UN and the churches that contributed the tools and nets to make it happen. We created an extra source of income for the fishermen, and they were all very happy. I was totally pleased with the outcome of these projects, which were gaining momentum in improving the lives of our people. My negotiation with the military to let all refugees have the freedom to go out of the camp daily to shop, to sightsee, to go to a cinema as long as they were back inside the camp by 5:00 p.m. was getting a stamp of approval. The dark side of it was that those who did not follow the rules would be disciplined. They would be placed in the "monkey house" (a barbed-wire cage)! But it was a fair game, I thought.

I had been spending a lot of time at the offices, meeting after meeting, and had very little time for my family. But my wife understood my dedication and commitment to public life and never had any complaints. Besides, she had her little sister, Nhan, to give her a hand to run the family affairs from cooking to laundry. My two sons, Lam and Tuan, were in her good care as well, and I am grateful for that. She was always kept busy doing all kinds of household work. Whether she liked it or not, her name, Nhan, which means "leisure" in Vietnamese, was assumed to be a mistake, as we sometimes teased her.

I truly and wholeheartedly enjoyed the work I was doing for

the fellow refugees and for the camp. In serving them, I was somehow reminded and inspired by what Rabindranath Tagore, a Bengali poet, says in his poems:

ZZZZZ

"I slept and dreamed that life was joy,
When I awoke, I saw life was service,
And when I acted, behold! Service was joy."

ZZZZZ

I then saw a need for having a canteen for the camp, which was an opportunity to bring in income to fund social services and educational programs for the camp. I ran that by the committee and Lt. Pagaduane, and the idea was immediately translated into a small shop, utilizing the building space adjunct to the administration building. The mini store was set up, and voila! We sold everything from beer, soft drinks, snacks, and coffee to cigarettes directly to our refugee customers right inside our camp. My wife and her friend Phan volunteered their expertise in the grocery business to do the buying and selling. They would go downtown on the local tricycle to the market every morning to make their purchases and come back into the camp before noon. We had two men, one middle-aged, Uncle Tu, and one in his early twenties, Brother Hien, as we called them, who eagerly worked as volunteers, devoting their time and energy to provide service to customers and prepare food on the side.

Business was very good, I must say. The store, which had eight hundred square feet of floor space, was always busy from late morning to late evening. At a table, a customer refugee could enjoy a hot bowl of ramen noodles, whose steam permeated and faded into the air; a happy face of a youngster who came for a cracker snack; and a French-style black coffee leisurely dripped into a glass with white, condensed milk waiting at the bottom to merge and mix. A bottle of cold beer with sweat beads running down the side sat on the table, which, along with soft music intermixed with giggles and laughter, came from those who came to make the best of their time in the camp. All of these came about because our volunteers were determined to make things happen. I was so proud of them.

The bookkeeping and accounting were being done by one of the committee members who used to work as controller for the former government in Vietnam. Everyone involved worked together so well, so harmoniously, that they created a friendly environment for the refugees to stay and enjoy the services inside the camp. The business for this canteen was growing and doing so well that the vendors from the local areas outside the camp began to file complaints to the Western Command. However, we had every reason to be busy. We sold our goods at a very low profit margin to help our fellow refugees and keep the profits in our camp. There was a little politics being played here. The UNHCR had been informed of this venture and seemed happy with the progress. The churches also recognized our efforts to benefit the life of the refugees. The recognition of our success went to the military command. It was their credit. Who would want to rock the boat?

Life of the refugees here in the camp was getting better every day. On the social front, our soccer team from the camp had gone outside to compete with the local teams and won every time. Believe me, they loved the competition, and I must say, soccer was in our blood. We were undefeated. Mr. Ngo, a former major of the army, a delightful middle-aged man in charge of the social services, spent endless hours pushing for cultural exposures. Besides movie nights inside the compound, his teams of dancers and singers performed at the local Holy Trinity College, which won praises from the school officials as well as the local community. His effort here was to make a cultural connection to the world outside of the camp and to keep our traditions alive. I truly enjoyed him and working with him. His destination was Canada.

Mr. Vuong Dinh Thanh, a former police officer, was in charge of the internal security team and pushed his program of physical fitness. His taekwondo class was gaining momentum and popularity. I felt that I was blessed with all talented men who helped me in their fields of expertise in serving our fellow men and women with their love and dedication. His assistant, Mr. Luong, who came on my boat, was a former officer, a major in the Vietnamese National Police Forces. He brought in his own wealth of expertise to serve. One incident took place on a Sunday afternoon. It was sunny and rather warm and quiet day at the camp. There was a young man in his late twenties who was escorted by a guard and a security person to the office. Mr. Thanh and Luong were also at the office when I was paged to come over. Before I was told of any charges against this person, I felt the seriousness of the problem. The grim expression on everyone's face and the air in the office made me feel the gravity of something to unfold.

It began with a complaint from an elderly couple who lived not too far from the camp. They let this young man into their home one day, and out of their kind hearts and their hospitality, they asked him to stay for lunch, which he did, and he befriended them. After lunch, these folks showed the man the house. There was not much to show except a camera they had owned for a long time, and according to them, it was of a very high quality and was worth a lot of money. They also said that this young man had shown much interest in it and examined it thoroughly. Later on that day, after this young fellow had left, they discovered that their camera was gone. No one else other than this man had come inside the house, and therefore, he must be the guilty one.

How could it be? I wondered about this whole thing and was a little confused about the charges. Here was a young person who said that these folks were like his parents, who were so very kind to him, fed him, and yes, they did show him the camera. But he claimed he had nothing to do with its disappearance. He said repeatedly that it would be like stealing it from his own parents and that he would never do that unless he were an animal. After listening to his argument, defending himself very emotionally and vehemently, I told the guard that this matter needed further investigation and I would let his superior know as soon as I found out more about this. As the guard left the office to go back to his duty at the gate, I asked my security officers, Mr. Thanh and Mr. Luong, for their opinions and their judgment on this man and his charges. I told them what I had thought about it as I had listened to his story. He was not the one who stole that camera. There must be something else we did not know. I wanted to believe this elderly couple, whose kindness was shown beyond doubt, but the young man here would not have the heart to hurt them by taking their precious thing from their home.

But Luong told me that this young man was the guilty one and he would soon prove it to me. Lo and behold, within two days, I was asked to come to the office to see this young man, and the camera was on the table. He admitted to the theft. In disappointment, I let the officers handle the charges, the penalties, and at the same time, I looked at Luong in awe, admiring his skills, his intelligence. How he did that I would never know. By the way, he and Mr. Thanh both were accepted for the US program, and they would be on the manifest in a few months.

I had been staying in my coconut palm leaf hut for a while now with my family and was so busy with my work at the office. I had totally forgotten the miserable life that I had experienced months and years before. One afternoon, however, during the siesta period of the whole camp, I dozed off on my bamboo mat next to my kids. The whole scenario of my unpleasant experiences with the new regime was relived in a nightmare. Being chased by the soldiers and being handcuffed came alive, as did the imprisonment, the labor camps, the beatings, and the sounds of gunfire bullets splashing the water right next to my boat. All of these detailed incidents played back into my dreamlike state like videotape full of action. I was half-awake, and this played in my subconscious mind to the extent that I felt I was really on the run again. Being so scared, I woke up from the nap. As I opened my eyes and gradually saw the palm leaf roof above me, I slowly realized that I was now safe in the refugee camp. It was just a dream. What a relief!

As I said earlier, when I was picked for this job, I had not had any formal classes or training in the field of leadership. It just happened that I was open and willing to learn from the everyday situations I encountered. There was an incident in which a young man was under disciplinary measures for domestic violence. He had beaten up his wife and created a commotion at his living quarters, and as result, he was placed in the monkey house (an open-cage jail) not too far from the gate, where there was an armed guard who could watch the inmate all the time. It was a Sunday afternoon. Lt. Pagaduane and I had a talk at the office about the affairs of the camp, and we both agreed on the progress we had made to improve the life here in the refugee camp. It was a brief, informal self-evaluation for both of us, and we were somewhat content with what we had accomplished. We were both in a good mood, and because of this, we decided to release the inmate from the monkey cage, who had been there for over a week. As the decision was made, I asked for Mr. Thanh to inform him of the decision. The man was then set free out the cage.

A few hours later, late in the evening, gunshots were heard from the gate to the office of the camp. The guard had discovered the inmate was gone from the monkey house, and now he wanted him back inside the barbed-wire cage. Obviously, his boss had not informed him of our mutual decision, and I was asked to come over to talk to this mad gunman. At the scene, I explained to him what had transpired between his officer in charge and me. But he was adamant that the man had to be put back in the monkey house. Frustrated at his unreasonable attitude, I looked at him in the eyes and flatly told him that I could not go back on my word, my decision, and as far as I was concerned, this man was free of any charges and was also free from going back to the cage. If he was not happy with that, he could put me in the cage instead. Just as soon as I had finished saying that, it seemed as though thousands of voices collectively in thunders said "No, no" repeatedly. In fact, within minutes, the refugee population swelled into hundreds to protect and support me just in case I was bullied. Facing the unbeatable danger, the guard angrily left the scene and went back to his duty post at the gate. After the "leadership show," I got pats on my back from my security people and my colleagues for my courage in action, or you may say leadership 101 in real life. The following morning, the lieutenant came to apologize for the incident, a miscommunication, and the mess that he had created. I told him that I was glad the guard did not push hard enough to put me in the monkey house. In his apologetic gesture, shaking his head, he smiled and said, "Sorry; I am sorry, Mr. Le."

After this incident of confrontation with the rifled guard, I sometimes asked myself a question, and it was the very question I had many times, silently, mentally, asked myself, as if I were communicating with my other invisible self: "How did you do that?"

As you may have guessed, I would never have the answer. But in my heart, I knew it all well. It was the very same spirit that kept me calm and helped me through when I was caught by the two cops just before my trip and the very same one that guided me through the storm and lifted me over many obstacles in life. In fact, it was just a few days before this incident, just a beautiful, sunny day and a rather warm day too. I decided to take half a day off from work and went home early. As I got home, I felt a bit of guilt, as I had not spent much time with my boys except in the evening and bedtime when each of them would crawl next to me and I would have them in each of my arms as we would all fall asleep. I asked them if they would like to go to the beach for a swim.

They were jumping and screaming with joy as if they had been dreaming and waiting for this moment. Within minutes we were at the large pond adjacent to the beach, and we decided to get wet here first. With just my shorts on, I had Lam on my back and Tuan in my arms as I walked into the water. It was nice and warm, the water was a little murky, but it was nonetheless good for a dip on a warm day. There were a few swimmers scattered out at the beach but none at that particular pond. The three of us, father and sons, were holding tight on to one another and happily moving about in the water, laughing and having the time of our lives. Suddenly I lost my balance as I walked off a cliff into deeper water. God knew how deep and how big the pocket of the deep water was. All I knew was I had my kids hanging tight on me, bobbing up and down as I was trying to keep my feet moving as fast as I could to stay afloat. But with the weight of my kids on me, my energy drained quickly as I kicked my feet frantically to keep us up. I was exhausted. For minutes, we were down and up, up and down in the water, thinking surely we were going to be drowned here and no one would know to come to rescue us. Lam, hanging on my back, holding to my neck and crying, said in his native tongue, "Chet roi, minh chet roi, bo oi!" (Dad, we are going to die!)

In between a little air and lots of water in my mouth, I wanted to calm him but could not make it into words. A flash of thought came to me as a prayer: God help me; please give me the strength to protect my children. Please help us here. You have saved us, crossing the sea under the storm; please save us at this little pond.

I kept fighting for my life and that of my sons' lives in the water for seconds or minutes, but it seemed to be an eternity until my feet touched a solid spot. I stood on it, and I stayed there. Whew! It was then I gained my composure and took a deep breath, knowing that we were still alive. It was a scary event. With my boys still on me, I carefully moved my feet slowly on a rough, rocky platform inch by inch under the water, making sure that I would not fall into that pit again. By the time we got out of the water, I was completely exhausted but happy and glad that my boys were safe. What an event! What an experience! I almost lost my life and the lives of my children for such a mundane thing as swimming in a little pond. I then realized that at one side of this curtain of life, one is always at risk—risk of sudden death, risk of accidents, risk of being sick, risk of the risks themselves—and we all take life for granted. And on the other side, the beauty of life is expressed in many different ways, from infancy to childhood to a life of an adult. One can see the beauty in the innocence of a child, in the smiles of a baby, and in an act of kindness of the older person. These make life bright, meaningful, and appreciable.

In my case, I did cling to my life, fighting for the life of my children. The shock and the fear of being drowned still resided on their faces. I held them tightly in my arms and let the tears of gratefulness well up in my eyes. At the same time, I knew the feeling of guilt, the guilt of putting my sons at risk. The guilt of almost ending their lives was eating me away. I whispered in their ears that I was very sorry and kissed them as we began our walk home. The people heading to the beach in groups of threes, fours, and more would not know of the near-drowning experience that we had just had. They greeted us with their smiles, and I told them to be very careful swimming at the pond. I did not think anyone would have their kids on their back when swimming.

The sun was just about hiding behind the buildings as we were walking and talking, and before we knew it, we were home. My boys told their mom of the details of the incident that brought about a remark from her something like, "Be more careful next time." She was not a swimmer herself, and I promised myself to be very, very careful next time and all the time. After dinner, bedtime came, and as always, my boys clung to me. This time I held them tight with my tears of joy and gratefulness that we were alive.

Life continued to improve in this camp amid some unfortunate incidents. Some of the refugees came in with stories of their boats that encountered mechanical problems and depleted food supplies and water, which resulted in starvation. There were few survivors. This happened at the same time there were incident reports of unfortunate boat persons in other parts of South Pacific Ocean.

The most terrified ones were those who encountered Thai pirates when their boat trips were heading to the shorelines of Thailand. There were unforgettable memories of women being raped, tortured, and killed. These ruthless Thai pirates took the belongings, raped the women, young and old, and killed those who dared to resist them. The news of the killings from those who survived traveled back to Vietnam and to the United States and to other parts of the world. There was an international public outcry. The Vietnamese communities around the world immediately called on the United Nations to step in to save the lives of these unfortunate boat people. It took months under the pressure of the UN for the Thai government to finally clean up the mess of pirates at their waters.

I hoped some day there would be a report or a sort of a tally of the number of those who made it and those who were unfortunate and lost their lives to the sea. This would help us all appreciate life and therefore live to the best of it. This reminds me of a beautiful saying from Mahatma Gandhi, who said, "Live as if you would die tomorrow; learn as if you live forever."

I saw local villagers, most of them women, who every morning roamed outside the fence behind my barracks with their baskets filled with local fruits. They bartered with the refugees inside the fence for food such as rice or meat. This practice was not allowed and was against the rules and regulations set by the Western Command, but I had no heart to turn them away. These villagers outside the fence and those of us inside were from the same fabric of life, the same economic conditions, or they were perhaps worse off than us. We were both leaning on each other to survive. The people of the Philippines, the villagers, in particular, were so generous in their hearts and in their deeds. This went back to the first night when the fisherman brought me to the village under the heavy rain of the storm. The village chief himself and his family opened their door to welcome me, fed me, and clothed me until I found my family. The fisherman labored his way to safely bring me to his mooring dock and handed me over to the chief to care for me. All of this was done out of their hearts, and none of them expected anything in return. This is called "kindness in action," and it should be contagious and must be practiced by every human being.

During the course of running the camp, I was every now and then presented with some bills for my signature to acknowledge the receipt of goods for the refugees at the camp. This was a procedure for reimbursement from the United Nations to the Western Command for the expenses incurred for operating the camp. I questioned the items I had never seen or received and were of a significant amount. But it was explained to me this way. "Mr. Le, the monies spent on entertaining the delegations from embassies, the hotel rooms, the dinners, and so on so forth for our guests, it has to come from somewhere, not from the military budget of the Western Command."

Now I understood the nature of this money business about which I had never been told, and of course, at this point, I did not want to rock the boat. My people had never been happier at the camp. They, unlike those in the past, enjoyed freedom just like the normal local people. They were free to go shopping, sight-seeing, and visiting, except that they had to be inside the camp within the agreed time frame. The food supply—the basics, such as rice, fish, meat, and vegetables—were at an acceptable quantity and quality, all of which were funded by the United Nations and brought in by a local contractor. Besides, the fishermen of the camp could have their time like the old days in Vietnam. They could go fishing at night and sell their catch in the morning for cash; it was theirs to keep and spend as they wish. I certainly did not want to see all these privileges go away, so I considered it a tradeoff.

I had been chairman for a little over two months, and it meant that there was only a month left of my chairmanship. The UNHCR commissioner, Mrs. Schmidt, had begun asking me to stay for one more term. I told her I would love to, but for the sake of my children, I'd rather not. They had wasted a lot of their time already, and we needed to get going so that they could catch up with their schooling in the US. I did thank her for her support and her recommendation for extending my term. At the same time, I felt a bit flattered by her trust and confidence. She said she totally understood my situation and my position but thought she wanted to give it a try anyway. She also asked for my advice concerning my replacement. I told her I had had someone in mind, but I needed more time to think it over to see if it would work for him and for her.

At one of the meetings of my council and staff, Mr. Qua Ba Le, a former attorney at law from Saigon who had been accepted for the Canada program, seemed to see the urgency of the situation. He was very concerned that the military would take over control of the camp once I had left. He advised that somehow, someway, I must create a feeling of my presence, even a false one, after my departure from the camp. The mood of the meeting that morning was solemn, and I felt moved by the suggestion and by their support for me. I told them that I could not in my most creative world think of any ways of doing that except to continue to do what I had been doing and cultivate a more solid relationship with the military personnel, especially with the officer in charge, Lt. Pagaduane. At the same time, I would reinforce the notion that once I was no longer around here, they needed to continue the same level of kindness toward all the refugees. The committee went even further by suggesting keeping my voice on the air such as that of the "English on the air" twice a day, morning and evening. Once again, I felt somewhat flattered and honored at the same time. I told them they should not be worried about the change. It could only be better, and they should stay focused on the positive outcome from the positive thinking and serving one another.

ON THE MANIFEST

Tom and Mary of the US Embassy confirmed my US acceptance and stated that my family and I should be on the manifest to travel to José Fabella, a transit camp, within a month for medical procedures. They both had been my very good friends, and with this friendship, I had been able to help lots of cases that were otherwise unqualified for the US program.

As time was approaching for my departure from the camp, it became a pretty emotional each day. My friendship among the refugees had become so strong that it would be uneasy to break away. It was very hard to think that once you left there, it would be almost impossible to see each other again. We all would be spreading out, going different directions, as hosting countries had chosen us. One might go to the US or to Canada or Australia or France, and others to Spain and so on. We all knew in our hearts that this period of time staying in this camp lasted just a short while before we were taken to be resettled in faraway countries. Therefore, we determined we should make our stay more meaningful by opening our hearts, by extending our loving and caring to one another; and most of us had been doing just that. However, there were just a few individuals who could not fit into this harmonious living style due to psychological or personal problems. They then got into trouble, and as a result, they held grudges against those individuals who disciplined them on behalf of the camp administration. And rumors were that these individuals would take revenge against committee or council members once they arrived at the transit camp, José Fabella, in Manila. I personally treated rumors as rumors and did not let it bother me a bit.

At least three Chinese Vietnamese families who arrived at the camp months before I did asked me what their status was. They had also been interviewed and accepted for the US program; however, they had never been on the manifest to go. Every time the roster came, the names of those to be airlifted to Manila would be read over the PA system, but theirs had not been mentioned. It was a moment of anticipation, of joy, as well as disappointment for those who had been promised but never ever had anything happen. Their hope had come and gone over the months like the tide, like the waves of the sea that rise and flatten into the immensity of the water that they had come to know and experience as boat people. Hope and disappointment intermixed into their thinking and feeling as time passed by day by day. I promised them that I would definitely look into it when I got to Manila. Mary and Tom had asked me if I wanted to stop by to see them at the embassy, and I told them that I would be delighted to come when I got there. I told myself that it would be my mission to check this out with the help of these two friends.

D-DAY

The D-day quickly came to us. It was very emotional for me. It was not easy to say good-bye to those who all along supported me, cared for me, and advised me in my work. Colonel Cunanan came to say farewell on behalf of the Western Command. He wished all of my family the best, and I thanked him and the military personnel for all of their support and care for the refugees in the camp. Lt. Pagaduane, SSgt. Gomez, SSgt. Sabardo and I had a get-together in our canteen to exchange our mutual appreciation and gratitude to one another. I personally thanked every one of them for working with me and supporting me in my work as chairman to bring about the results now seen in the camp. I also wholeheartedly asked them to continue to support my committee and council and especially the next chairman of the camp. I personally recommended my dear friend Dr. Timothy Vo to Mrs. Schmidt of UNHCR to be the next chairman. And the same recommendation went to my military friends who also agreed to have him as my replacement. Dr. Timothy Vo had been working very hard along with me. His enthusiasm and dedication earned the respect of all in the camp. I was in awe of his talents, his knowledge of literature, of art and languages, and felt that he was the best choice for this position. I would never forget the incident in which he performed so well as an interpreter to the "second pope" who paid a visit to the camp. The holy man from the Vatican addressed the crowd of over two thousand refugees of different faiths in French, and Tim was there to convey the message of love and hope and his sympathy to our plight in our language so well, so fluently that it brought tears to our eyes.

Once we were on the road to the airport, the dust stirred up behind our vehicle pushed my camp, our camp, into the distance, and gradually it faded away. I knew that I would miss this place where I had met lots of people. I would treasure their friendship for many years to come. It was quite a mixed emotion, in which, on one hand, I wanted to get going to the US for the sake of my children, and on the other, I would miss my people at the camp. I knew that I couldn't have both.

A short flight brought us over to the Manila airport, where we were transported to the José Fabella refugee transit camp. It had been many years since I last flew on an airplane, and this time I did enjoy the flight. My kids did like it as well, for it was their very first flight. My family was prearranged to stay in the so-called "halfway home." It was a separate building from the main camp. It was quite nice with light beige walls and a cement floor, which was a big thing for my wife and the children simply because we were at the camp for almost a year on the dirt floor. Another surprise was a TV set in the corner ready for us to use. We thought that there must be some kind of special treatment reserved for us, because I would have never expected or dreamed of this being provided for a refugee. It was completely opposite what the rumors had said about the harsh treatment awaiting those who served in the office at the refugee camp in Palawan. At this moment as I was isolated in this building with just my family, I wanted to know how other boat people refugees lived in this transit camp. I would check this out as soon as I settled in. Outside the building, at the entrance, there were boxwood hedges and flowerbeds of roses and peonies in bloom as if welcoming us.

I soon found out that the one who was solely responsible for this TV set and special living arrangement was a lady guest who had come to the camp for a visit. She was one of the church ladies whose church was based out of Manila. After spending some time talking with me and other people at the camp, she told me that she would like to see me when I came to Manila. Of course, I had no way of letting her know of my date of arrival, let alone calling her. But she must have had a network that fed her the news of my coming to José Fabella. This was one of her touches of loving care. Later on the following day, she came to pay us a visit and said that she would like to take us for a visit to her place of residence some day. I thanked her for her thoughtfulness and her tender care and told her that my family would love to come to visit her but to please come to pick us up. With her gentle smile, she said, "Of course, I would not want you all to walk out here into the street to get hurt."

She asked us to let her know of anything we might need so that she could bring it over. After eight months living in the refugee camp and getting used to the conditions of getting by on a survival mode, I felt that we had plenty and did not know what else to ask for. We could only show her our appreciation for her kindness.

The following day, I came to the office to meet with the person in charge of the camp. He met me with his genuine touch of friendship, for he had heard about my arrival. He said he had been told about my service at the Palawan camp and would like to take care of me and hoped that I would give him a hand while I was in Manila. I told him I would not mind. I asked him about the rumors of vengeance on those who had served in the Palawan camp. He said there was some truth to it but that he would not tolerate that kind of practice in his camp, and he meant it. I now saw some of my people who had come earlier and were waiting to have medical exams. They all were so happy to see me, and I was very delighted to see them as well.

I was so very lucky. How to describe it, I do not know. Here is what happened. Mrs. Schmidt from the UN came for a visit, along with my friends Tom and Mary. They asked me if I would want to work at the embassy while in Manila. I told them yes, I would love to. The possibility of this offer had not crossed my mind. I had not even planned to have a job while waiting on the medical processing. They told me I could start any time I wished, but in the meantime, they wanted to show me around and take me to the embassy area where they worked.

Manila on this sunny Sunday morning was crowded and bigger than I had thought. The three Filipino amigos in my concentration camp had told me a lot about Manila, their capital city and hometown, but nothing in my mind could compare to this. The traffic, the cars, the buses were zigzagging at a dizzying speed. I was wondering about the traffic rules and traffic accidents, and then came the comment from Tom: "If you can drive in Manila, you can drive anywhere in the world."

I felt there was truth in his observation. It was noticeable that the people of the Philippines loved colors and decorations. The top of a bus, full of passengers inside, was loaded with baskets full of all kinds of fruits, ranging from mangoes and jackfruits to bananas. It had a mixture of bright colors painted on the sides; others had different patterns, but all were colorful and bright. I also noticed many midsized trucks painted burgundy red that had lots of chrome-color horns mounted on top and sides of the hood and were accented with stripes in white. I wondered if any of those horns actually added to the sound and noise to the traffic, which seemed generated by the continuous sounds of horns from the streams of vehicles.

After sightseeing, which included driving through the downtown and embassy areas, I was dropped off back at the camp. As they were leaving, they asked me if I could come to work the next morning so that they could send a taxi cab to pick me up. I was very happy to hear that and told them that I would be looking forward to seeing them at their office.

I told my wife and kids about the temporary job at the embassy and that I would start the next morning. They were all happy and said they were proud of me. I tried to hide my excitement and my anticipation about the job by watching a show on the black-and-white TV. It dawned on me that I had not seen and watched a TV show for years. I had not had this kind of luxury, for I had been busy working, making plans for this moment to happen.

I was seated on the cement floor with my back against the wall, and my kids were right next to me with their eyes on the TV screen, which was showing a Disney cartoon movie. They were totally into it. The coolness of the dark teal-colored floor, which was cleaned and mopped with wet towels just like we used to do back home so that we could lie down to have a nap on the warm day, brought me to the simple crystal-clear realization that I had been blessed in many ways, and I was counting my blessings. In this moment of reflection and meditation, I realized that in the past eight months, ever since I arrived at the camp, I had been immersed wholeheartedly in serving the community of my fellow refugees and hardly had much time for my family and myself as I did now. Losing and then finding my family during the storm, the near-drowning experience at the pond at the refugee camp, the acceptance of my family to the US program initiated by Mary and Tom, the love and trust from my fellow men at the camp, the loving care from the church lady who made this living arrangement for my family, and unnamed other things were sequences of blessings in my life. I could not help but silently say thanks to the divine God who watched over me every step of the way. I knew that not very long down the road I would be in the US to start my new life and I would no longer worry about the labor camp, imprisonment, and hatred toward the Communists. I wanted to begin at that very moment to end those kinds of feelings and to become a free man. I did not want to have them keep me in prison while I was here in the free world. This was a lesson I learned when reading a passage from a book saying that there were two men, both of whom had been in the Nazi concentration camp. They now saw each other at the market place. One asked the other if he remembered the old time in the Nazi camp where they were humiliated, mistreated, and faced other unpleasant things. The other answered in a very angry, unhappy voice, full of hatred, "How could I forget those days, those terrible things they did to us? I will never ever forgive them."

"Obviously," this man told him, "they still have you imprisoned for all these years."

There is a lesson here to learn about how to forgive and to forget. Forgiveness is a must, a moral and fundamental attitude to bring about freedom, and I was determined to erase those unpleasant experiences from my memory bank.

I woke up very early the next morning after a good five-hour sleep to make sure that I would have enough time to wash up and eat breakfast before the taxi came. My first day at work in the US Embassy would be exciting, I told myself. I made a mental list of what I needed to accomplish. I did not know what my wages would be or how many hours a day I would work or the number of days in a workweek. I did not know if there was enough work for me there until my departure to the United States. All of this did not concern me this moment. All I knew was that my excitement came from the notion that I had the job working at the US Embassy in the Philippines, where I was a refugee. It was a big thing to me. After all, it was also an opportunity for me to fulfill my commitment to check on the status of the three families to whom I made my promise.

It was a nice and cool morning when I arrived at the office where the sign "Joint Voluntary Agency" was nicely hung above the door. Mr. Applegate, the director of the agency, was expecting me and greeted me warmly. We had met once at the camp quite a while in the past. He then introduced me to his wife, who was also on staff at his office, as well as to the rest of his workers, most of whom were native people. I found that everyone was very friendly, and I felt comfortable in this working environment where I would be working for the next few weeks.

After a round of introductions and the tour of the office in the building, I asked Mr. Applegate if I could see the records of those who were currently still in Palawan and those who had left. He asked me what I had in mind. I told him the situation of those families who had been accepted for the US program for almost a year, and for some mysterious reasons, beyond anything I could possibly explain to them, they were still in the camp waiting impatiently to be called. With a doubtful look in his eyes, he asked me to come along with him to the office, which held the files and records and was located in the back of the building. I immediately asked him to let me look at the files of those who had already left, which had an "inactive" label. My reason for doing so was, first of all, the number of the files in the inactive box must be fewer than those active ones; therefore, it would take less time to do the checking and investigating.

Second, I had felt there was something fishy about the situation of these families, something out of the ordinary about the ways the accepted applicants were processed. I had noticed that the captain of my boat, who came to the camp the very same time I did, was called on the manifest with his family members to be airlifted only a few months after his arrival. And out they went to the United States. Almost everyone in the camp was surprised at how fast his case was processed and accepted. No one had any authority to look into that, and after all, no one really cared. We all wished them well, for they were the lucky ones. But time after time, these folks came to me, asking me why they had not been called. Everyone who arrived at the camp at the same time with them, one by one, had left the camp. Their frustration became my concern and suspicion, and I began to feel that there was a flaw in the processing system. I was here to find out very soon.

It took only seconds for me to point out to Mr. Applegate, my new boss, that the three folders bearing the names of the three refugees of Chinese origins belonged to those families who were currently staying at the camp. They should have been in the upper drawer with a label "Active." Instead, they were placed and kept in the bottom one, labeled "Closed" for those files, which belonged to the ones who had already left. He was in a state of shock at my discovery and wanted to have my assurance that what I had just discovered was not a mistake. I gave him my affirmation, my assurance that I had seen them every day at my camp until the day I left.

Telephone conversations began taking place, and the incoming phone rang off the hook to punctuate the gravity of the situation. I was never told the details of what had transpired. All I knew was I got a compliment from Mrs. Schmidt, who called from her UNHCR office, and the next move was to have these people flown to Manila on the next available flight. I thanked Mr. Applegate for allowing me to look into the cases of these poor families and said that I was very happy to work for him while in Manila. I did believe he was innocent of wrongdoing, but I almost wanted to mention to him that my boat captain had brought with him heavy sacks of gold. I thought I had scored a first victory on the first day at work. The Applegates treated me fairly well, and I enjoyed working with them. Every now and then, I went to the office of UNHCR to see Mrs. Schmidt to talk about the ways in which the life of the refugees at the camp could be improved.

The church lady, Mrs. Shihao, came over to pick us up for a trip to her home in the suburbs of Manila. Her kindness and the genuine openness of her children made us feel welcome to her place, which was well-trimmed and cared for. The simplicity of her life permeated her place of living. Large beige-colored walls were accented with one or two contemporary paintings of nature with a touch of family life. The furniture was light cherry in color, which beautifully contrasted with the walls; there were a minimum number of pieces. Passing through her kitchen, we were in the backyard of the house, where she grew all kinds of flowers that were blooming in the late-June sun. I had forgotten it was summer! She talked about her faith and her family, which had helped her through hard times when she lost her husband to heart failure. She shared and talked to us as if we were her family members. We felt close to her and her kids right in her place, even though we had known each other a short time. I guessed we had been connected at the quantum level but were unaware of it. She brought us home to the camp after she fed us lunch at her place. We were all blessed with her generosity and her kindness.

The life at José Fabella transit camp was uneventful until an evening long after my arrival. The flight bringing the refugees from the Palawan camp had arrived earlier in the day. Among the people were Mr. Qua Le, a former attorney at law, the committee member who had supported me tremendously in my administration, and his younger brother, Trang Le, who served well in the security team at the camp. They arrived nervous and fearing for their safety. It was late in the evening and getting dark. I was called and informed that these two brothers were in some sort of trouble with a gang. I got hold of the chairman of the camp and demanded that he provided protection for them. He and I went over to the building where there was commotion, to find out what had happened. It was all quiet when we arrived. The two brothers had also disappeared to some undisclosed hideout. No one could tell us anything of what had happened. I asked my friend if this sort of thing actually had happened in the past and if anyone had done anything about it. He said he was just a refugee like other refugees staying here, waiting for a short while before getting to be resettled in a third country. He had very little control over the refugee population in this camp, where it was deemed the last stop before freedom. I disagreed but said nothing, for my mind was with the two brothers and wondered where they were hiding and what needed to be done for them in the morning. I told my friend my concerns and asked him if he knew what to do to help them. He said he would do his best to protect them. Unlike the Palawan camp, this place did not have a fence, nor did it have guards or patrols. It was some sort of free zone where people could roam in and out. Anything could happen. Now I knew the reason for the rumors.

The next day, as we were scheduled for medical exams for everyone in my family at the medical processing center in the downtown area, I did not have time to find the brothers to talk to them. I wanted to make sure that I did everything I could so that they could feel safe while they were there. Sadly, with a busy schedule of working at the JVA office from dawn to dusk, I never had a chance to meet with them again before I departed for the US.

It was a long day at the medical center, from x-rays to lab tests to physical exams done on each of us. There were forms to fill out, and there was only one physician to take care of our group. It was a young female doctor, and I felt a bit uneasy being naked of her. I was surprised at myself for having that kind of began to talk to myself: "Silly, are you a chicken, or are a soldier?" I did not have much time to have that mental saga before she was cheerfully greeting me, and I was all I was again. The exams went well, as I behaved like a soldier, and she was a uniformed doctor. She gave me a clean bill of health and wished me luck in the US. We were all grateful for her service and her professionalism.

We left the medical building with bags full of envelopes of different sizes; x-rays were in large manila ones with all personal information boldly written on the outside. The smaller white envelope had lab test results for each member of my family. All of these were in individual plastic bags for each one of us, and as I was leaving the building, I felt as though we were just done shopping at the shopping center or at a mall and had bags full of stuff.

Our time in Manila was winding down so fast that it was time again to pack up our belongings and say good-bye to all the friends in JVA, UNHCR, and José Fabella. My life was getting richer and being blessed every day with all new friends. In the book *The Touch of Wonders* by Gordon Arthur, he says, "The more appreciated, the more is given." There is so much truth in it. Just the small, mundane things of everyday life matters can bring joy and appreciation if one can recognize it, and I was noticing every bit of it. I treasured the friendships I had made ever since I arrived at the camp. They became the rays of life that connected us months and years after I settled in America. The hugs and the handshakes, the silent and spoken words from all those friends, made our leaving a dramatic one. Tears welling up in our eyes became contagious to the others.

UNITED STATES OF AMERICA

At last we were at the Manila International Airport, which was larger than I could have imagined. I could see all kinds of air-crafts of different sizes from different airlines, all of which I was not familiar with. I was told a Boeing 747, a giant airplane, was the one we were going to be flying on. However, I could not figure it out which one it was. To me they were all very big, even at a distance. As soon as we got off the bus, we were led into the terminal for checking in. The driver, a local man in his thirties, was also the person responsible for getting us boarding passes. He was a kind and pleasant man, helping us with the luggage and our belongings to check in, which was a long process and time consuming. We thanked him for his patience and well-done services and bade him farewell. We were given nametags that were then pasted onto our shirts. The instructions detailed in the refugee travel booklet definitely helped me a lot at this point in time. "Always ask for help if you need help," it says in the book, and I would follow it to the T. We stayed close to each other while waiting for our flight to make sure that we all would be boarding at the same time and none would get lost and none would get in trouble.

It was a bright, sunny day, July 17, 1980. It marked another land post and another benchmark in my life to a better future for my family. It had been almost a year since I left on my boat and escaped from my homeland. It was on the night of the twelfth of September of 1979, and I did not feel as if it had been close to a year on my calendar. I had been busy engaging in many activities at the camp in Palawan, in Manila, and today, I was leaving it all behind. I was now all to myself, having time for my family. My boys were dressed in fairly nice clothes and were sitting right next to me. They looked quite handsome and happy. They had lost a few years of their youthful time outside of the school system, and now there was a lot for them to catch up on once they got into school in the US. But I knew my boys would not have any problem to excel, and they would have all the future waiting ahead for them. After all, they were the reason we endured so much and risked so much. Now it would be up to them to learn and provide a future for their children, our grandchildren.

There were so many people, so many travelers passing by us. Some carried their bags; others pulled their luggage on the tile floor. They all dressed differently, and they must have come from different countries; some took their time and seemed to enjoy the now, casting their eyes and smiling at us, and others dashed by or ran as if they were about to miss their flight. The loudspeakers on the PA system seemed busy all the time making announcements in different languages: English, Chinese, French, and the native Tagalog. They announced flight arrivals and departures or paged in an urgent tone of voice the ones who were about to miss their flights or even helped missing persons locate their parties. I was quite amazed at the foot traffic of the passengers, the hustle and bustle of the workers, and the noises of people talking and laughing and the crying of the children being dragged by adults. All of this seemed to underly the chaos of life in this airport terminal. At the same time, I understood the system was sophisticatedly designed to have everything in working order. Flights were landing, and flights were taking off; the people seemed to be zooming in different directions but arrived at their designated locations. I was in awe and in appreciation of what was being offered.

As we boarded the aircraft, I was amazed at the size of it. Row after row of seats were nice and clean and were in a light burgundy color. We were guided to our seats by the flight attendants, who had been previously informed of our refugee status. They were very helpful as they showed us how to use the seat belts and adjusted the light controls above our heads. The air conditioning was a little on the cold side for my children, so they helped take care of that by handing us blankets. They showed us how to use headphones to listen to music. At last they showed us the use of a service button in case we needed them. I appreciated the information, the instructions, as I had never been on the aircraft of this size. For the rest of my family, this was their first flight in their life. My kids, Lam and Tuan, two of my brothers and a sister-in-law, Quang, Thi, and Nhan, as you can guess, were excited about flying. They said this giant airplane was bigger than their house. I did not know which of their houses they were referring to, the one in Vietnam or the one in the refugee camp they had just left last month.

It was a full flight, and a long one to the United States. The next stop would be in Honolulu, Hawaii, our port of entry to the US, where the screening of all entries would begin. Before taking off, the flight attendant went over the safety procedures, showed us how to use the seat belts, and advised us to follow the instructions in case of emergency. I then whispered the instructions in Vietnamese to each member of my family to make sure all understood.

A few minutes after we were airborne, I knew we were flying over and crossing the sea again, except we were hundreds times safer and faster. Since it was an international flight, meals were served and a choice of drinks was also offered. We all enjoyed the taste of the new food and drink, and besides, we were hungry. I knew we could use some food while waiting in the terminal, but I could not afford the airport prices. Therefore the hunger was to be accepted. We were used to the circumstances.

Now everyone in my family had dozed off to the faint humming of the aircraft flying at hundreds of miles an hour. I hoped they had a good rest and beautiful dreams, the dreams of better days ahead of us, the dreams of a bright future for my children.

The flight attendants in their light blue-colored uniforms shuttled back and forth with a tray of cups in one hand and the teapot in the other and gently offered their service to their passengers who were wide awake. The lights were now off inside the aircraft except the reading lights from the overhead for those who were reading. From where I was seated, with the dim light, I could see other people with blankets on their shoulders beginning to sleep. My mind went back to the early time when I was on the last flight from North Vietnam to South by French aviation in 1954. I was seven years of age, a little boy. Here I was in 1980, boarding a 747 to the United States by a US-made airplane at the age of thirty-three, an adult with a family. In both cases, the sizes of the aircraft were significantly different; one was about three times the other, but my status was the same: a refugee seeking freedom from totalitarian regimes. The first time, as a young boy, I was under the care of my parents, and now as adult, I cared for my children. They were now right next to me, one on each side, sleeping like babies, peacefully. I could now see the future for them, or to be exact, I could see their future beginning with this flight. They would have the summer to spend and become familiar with the new life in the United States, and when the summer was over, school would begin, and they would be right into it. They would probably have a little difficulty with language barrier, but within weeks, they should do just fine. I had read the reports on children from immigrant families who generally did amazingly well in many subjects, even excelled in the first few months of school. I looked at the handsome faces of my boys and silently told them that they would have my love and total support to excel. I had so much to be thankful for.

I was awakened when the light was turned on, and I heard the announcement from the captain that our aircraft would be encountering a short period of turbulence, that all were required to return to our seats, and seatbelts were to be fastened properly. Just as soon as the announcement was finished, the aircraft shook a little; then a sudden drop of altitude of the aircraft caused concerns among first-time flyers like those of my family. My boys squeezed my hands as if to ask, "Daddy, we are okay, right?" I held them tighter and gave them a look of assurance that we should be fine and should be out of this bad weather shortly. As matter of fact, we did not stay in that pocket of air for very long. The captain kept us abreast of the weather conditions as well as the distance to the destination. We sighed with relief, for we did not want any unpleasant surprises.

Sunny Honolulu welcomed us at last. The giant plane landed smoothly after announcements and preparations were made. I was in awe of the skills of the pilots combined with the modern technology that allowed it to happen. As the aircraft was taxiing in, we were asked to "stay seated with the seatbelts fastened until the aircraft has come to a complete stop and the captain has turned off the fasten seat belt sign." I noticed that this large congregation did what they were told. Once it was time to exit the plane, we gradually, one by one, stood up and grabbed our belongings from the overhead compartments and slowly emerged into the flow of passengers headed to the door of the aircraft like an ant follows the one ahead of him. Those of us who were refugees were asked to have our personal papers handy as we were led into a separate building for immigration processing. It was quite a relief to be able to stretch, to walk after a long period of time sitting (without even going to the restroom during the flight).

The process was rather lengthy because of our status. Many forms needed to be filled out and checked thoroughly by the officials, for here was our port of entry into the United States. Not only the legal forms, but also the health documents had to be validated. When everything was checked out, we legally entered the United States of America, and the officials greeted us, "Welcome to the US. You are officially in America!" What a feeling! The sun was high in the clear Honolulu sky, with a few white clouds drifting lazily high above. The breeze from the sea brought the coolness and a faint touch of familiar algae salty scent, the one I had grown to love. The birds of paradise showed off their colors; the birds were singing and playing in and out of the trees outside the building; all seemed to join together to congratulate us: "Welcome to the United States of America!"

It was late in the evening when our plane landed at the San Francisco International Airport, where we were transported to an overnight transit facility near the airport. We were all worn out by the long flights and the long custom checks at the port of entry in Honolulu. Upon arrival at this facility, we were served fried rice with a touch of soy sauce that made the meal delicious and memorable. Someone must have known that we, the refugees, the displaced people, were very hungry and simple food such as fried rice would keep us happy, and it surely did. We were then, after dinner, shown the rooms for our night's rest. Early in the morning, we were to continue to our final destination, Chicago, where our cousin Duc and his family resided. We knew that we would have two more airports to take off from and to land before we arrived at our cousin's home. It was going to be a long day ahead of us, so we'd better get a lot of rest. I checked to make sure everyone had everything they needed for the night, and off I went to sleep.

I woke up early the next morning to a knock on the door to our room. It was the guard to make sure we got up in time for our flight to our destination. We immediately got ourselves moving, showering, cleaning up, and getting ready for the new day on the go. Once we were at the airport terminal to check in with the help of the airline worker who had been informed about our situation and status, we zoomed through all check-in procedures without any difficulties. While waiting for boarding, which would be taking place in about half an hour, my children asked me how much longer before we got to Chicago. I told them what the estimated time of arrival would be, provided that everything went smoothly with the schedule. I noticed that there were lots of services and care rendered on our behalf to get us from where we were to where we were going to be. It was a great, well-coordinated collective effort by all agencies and organizations to orchestrate this humongous plan to bring us, the refugees, to our final destinations, whether the United States or elsewhere in the world. Not only did they provide the logistical means, but also the food, the drink, and psychological support to make sure that we were able to function healthily and normally and enter into the mainstream of the new society. I felt that I had been blessed and was indebted to the society, to the governments, and to the whole of humanity for their love and kindness. The social workers, the airline attendants, the guards, all went above and beyond their duty to guide us and to make sure that we, step by step, got to where we were supposed to be.

The Denver airport greeted us with sunshine. It was just a beautiful day, and there was almost two-hour layover before our next flight to Chicago. We were inside the terminal waiting. The airline attendants told us not to wander too far off from the counter, for they did not want to spend time looking for us in case we got lost. They, I thought to myself, should not be worried because first, we did not want to get in trouble with anybody; second, we were not energetic enough to do any exploring at this time. We were so anxious to see our cousins and their family in Chicago. We were longing for a traditional meal of rice and fish and vegetable soup. We decided to kill time around the counter, looking at different aircraft outside of the windows, watching the landings and the take-offs of many giant iron birds at this busy airport. The travelers were all over inside the terminal; they were moving from and to different directions and seemed always in a hurry as if they were not having enough time to get to where they wanted to go. It seemed that every place and airport I had been to thus far was getting better and better in terms of architectural construction and interior design. I favored the design taste in the US over Manila's, which was a bit too colorful as opposed to the US décor, a touch of simplicity, as I noticed.

CHICAGO, THE HEARTLAND OF AMERICA

At the O'Hare International Airport in Chicago, our cousins were waiting for us at the terminal as we were strolling down the aisle. It was a very, very happy moment for all of us to be able to see each other again in this faraway land. They all looked so healthy and younger and much different than we remembered. The weathered suntan-dark skin of the old days of tropical dusty Saigon was now transformed with a nice softer one of Chicago of America. It had been almost five years since we last saw each other in Saigon. What I noticed and was impressed by was that the younger ones were talking to each other in English, not in Vietnamese, and appeared very American.

On the way home, after picking up our luggage and fitting everyone into their minivan, we talked about our trip and our flight from the Philippines. We talked about the old days in Vietnam and how we had missed their boat from their house to the US Navy ship that was out in the South China Sea at the end of the Saigon government era. In the middle of our stories and before we knew it, we had arrived home.

It was July in Chicago. When we got out of the vehicle, it was a little warm and humid. It felt as if I was in Saigon in the old days where summer was always humid, warm, and sticky. It was late in the afternoon, and my cousin's wife, Van, or Bich Van (pronounced *big van,* as a way of teasing her), had prepared a very traditional meal for all of us. It was more like a feast than a casual family dinner. From veggie soup to fish and pork and beef, all were prepared and cooked in Vietnamese style. It was a happy and delicious reunion dinner, and everyone enjoyed it very much. Cousin Van was known for her excellence in cooking and managing. She has always been cheerful and generous to all of us. We all thanked her and her family for sponsoring us and taking care of us while we were here in the US, at least for the time being. We adults talked about the past and the future while the kids got together and had their own good time, playing games and watching movies.

We went to bed early, for we were pretty exhausted from the traveling. I had a full schedule ahead of me for the next few days. I needed to see different government agencies for the refugee programs to search for a job and housing. I wanted to be independent from the relatives. They had been kind enough to sponsor us to come to start our new life here in the US. I was determined not to ever be a burden to them and a liability to the government. I wanted to make my American dream come true and to become a contribution to my new society. Somewhere, somehow, I read a beautiful line in a book that says, "When you get up in the morning, you should bask yourself in the notion of being a contribution." I just loved it, and I was beginning with it.

Cousin Van had made my appointment early in the morning, and I wanted to be there half an hour before my appointment. The traffic was not terribly bad, as I had been told, and we got to the office a bit too early, but they were all happy to see me anyhow. They all congratulated my family and me on the success of our journey to the United States and were happy to assist us in every way possible to make sure that we would continue our success into the mainstream of America.

They asked me what I would like to do, or to be exact, if I would be willing to do anything to bring income to the family. Of course, I told them I would be happy to do anything and everything to earn a living and support my family. They all seemed to be very happy with our direct communication and even more with the direct and firm response from me. In a conversation with my close friends and family members at the beginning of my planning for escape, I often said that I would be happy, be willing, to do anything, even the lowest-paying jobs and the ones involving hard labor. I would be satisfied as long as I could enjoy the air of freedom, could see the opportunity for everyone in the family and the future for my children. The irony is, as I found out not long after my arrival, the jobs that were deemed to be laborious, socially graded at the bottom, and low-paying in Vietnam were the high-paying ones in the US. Plumbing is a perfect example. So it helped to be open and take whatever came. I love what Jalaluddin Rumi, a thirteenth-century mystical poet of Persia who was born in Afghanistan, says in his poem: "Take sips of this divine wine being poured, never mind the dirty cup which you are given." He says it all to me in such a profound way.

The USCC office here had all of my personal history. The UNHCR and JVA of the US Embassy in Manila had given them everything they had overseas. I just had to reconfirm with them what they now knew. There were forms to fill out for my job search. Finally, with their blessing and on behalf of those good-hearted charitable souls, the director of the organization cheerfully handed me a check for $650 with kind words of congratulations. It was a large, light blue business-size check printed with black ink. The figure, the number, the dollar amount, and the wording of the amount represented a concept of monetary value that was so vague, so foreign to me for the very simple reason that I had never had a paycheck, had never seen one in thirty some years of my life. All monetary transactions I had ever had, be it in business or from employment, were all in forms of cash. One might be surprised or even wonder how in the world, a thirty-two-year-old man like me had never had a bank account, had never written or seen a check. But it was true, as it was that I, as many other Vietnamese, had never been exposed to the situation in which monetary transactions required checks.

I was deeply moved by the fact that the USCC had done so much for my family from sponsoring us to come, to help us with money to start our new life in the new land. I told the director of the agency how much I appreciated their efforts and the care they had given us and promised to use their caregiving money wisely or even multiply it many, many times.

As I was leaving and saying good-bye to the staff, they told me they would love to have me working for them at the office but needed to see if they could get the funds for the new position. In the meantime, they would keep their eye open for any job opening in the community, and they would let me know.

While staying at our cousins,' I was out on the hunt for jobs every day. I did not know that I was competing against a big pool of unemployed workers in different segments of the market. Many days after looking from dawn to dusk, I would come home with no better news of employment. The summer heat of Chicago did not help my situation a bit during the day, and in the evening, the worst came with the depressing news of the national economy on all the TV stations. And not too encouragingly, the rate of unemployment kept climbing up locally; I was discouraged. At one point, my cousins comforted me and suggested that if worse came to worst, I could always apply for public assistance, welfare. But I had promised myself to not ever become a burden or a liability to anyone, including the government. I had come this far, overcoming the hardships of labor camp and the dangers of sea. Handouts were not a choice, at least at this point in time.

Some of our cousins' friends came up with the suggestion that I should take advantage of this initial allowable time when one is not forced into employment and attend the two-year vocational training programs offered at the community college. There were programs in computer programming, electronics, heating, and air conditioning. All of this sounded enticing, but my family would have to depend on public assistance, which was not an option for me.

One week had gone by quickly, while I was anxious about

getting myself a job and finding a place for my own family. I got a phone call from one of my friends, a former student at the refugee camp in the Philippines. Before leaving the camp, we always exchanged phone numbers with those whom we would love to stay in touch with. This man was one of them. Manh Tran, Thu Anh, his wife, and his little boy, Dung, were very close to me while in the camp. Manh called me to see how I was doing and if I would consider moving to Mountain View in California, where he said it was nice and warm, just like the climate in Vietnam. After we talked about the new life in America, about the job market in where he was living, I told him that I was interested in that option of moving to California but would like to talk it over with my wife and the cousins. It did not take much to convince all of them my choice of moving was a good one because California offered nice, sunny weather almost year-round and a better chance of employment. And at the end of our second week in the United States, we were ready to move to Mountain View, California, where we actually began our new life in the United States of America.

Once again, we bade farewell to our loved ones and continued on our quest for a better life. Greyhound bus was the only choice we could afford. We used a big chunk of the money given by the USCC to purchase the tickets for our family, and the remainder was for expenses on the road.

It was a long ride on the bus, which covered thousands of miles from Chicago to the bay area of northern California. It was a full ride to begin with, but the seats got emptier at each stop, and we took advantage of the space to stretch our feet or even lie down for a nap. The bus made numerous stops along the way either to switch drivers or to rest. At each station we could buy some food snacks or drinks between stops. To save and to make sure whatever money we had left was enough for our minimal expenses of the trip, we brought with us some homecooked foods such as rice and sesame seeds roasted in salt and sugar. A small basket of bananas and apples was also added to our food stock. We bought very little food during our bus ride, except when the kids begged for hamburgers with cheese and French fries and their newly acquired favorites of Pepsi and Coca-Cola. At the end of our bus ride, we ended up with fourteen dollars when we arrived at the Mountain View Greyhound bus station. The ride was not bad compared to what we had been through coming to America. The scenery, the landscape, the freeways, and the traffic were all completely fresh to our memories. My seat was next to the window, which allowed me to see and enjoy the beauty of the American natural landscape. The weather was just beautiful, with sunshine most of the time. I felt blessed that I was alive and able to absorb the beauty of the tree-lined forests, the magnificence of the green grass hillsides, and the stretch of mountains far away.

Inside the bus there were people from all walks of life: a few blacks, some with a Hispanic background, and the majority were white. After a while on the same ride together, people would somehow strike up a conversation to break the ice, to become friends, especially with the ones sitting right next to you. That was my case. The man in the seat behind me was in his early forties, all by himself, and was very quiet except a smile or a nod here and a nod there when our eyes met. I decided to become the icebreaker by saying hello to him. He returned with a, "Hello, *bon jour*," which was followed by a flow of French. He said he was visiting from Quebec, Canada, and felt helpless or even intimidated amid English-speaking people. I could relate to what he said. With my broken French and his very little English, we managed to understand each other through universal language, and at the end of our trip, my hands were a bit tired!

We were happily greeted by our friends at the bus station in Mountain View and taken to their house, which was not too far from the station. The reunion moment for all of us was incredibly joyful. The time in the refugee camp had brought us close together as brothers and sisters, and when we parted, we did not know if we would ever meet again, and here we were. We celebrated and talked about our experiences of our trip to America.

The house was a two-bedroom ranch house with one bath.

He and his younger brother's family each stayed in one of the bedrooms. We would have the living room, the newcomers.

The first few days of our squeezing in seemed to be at the borderline of everyone's comfort zone. All of us realized that it would take some time to understand and to get along. But to live in a very tight space with two bedrooms and a small living room for three families for a long period of time was almost impossible, as I discovered shortly afterward. It would be okay if it were in the refugee camp, but not here now in America. The situation deteriorated, as the two sisters-in-law did not get along, and the air in the house was so thick, so heavy, and unfriendly that we would only come home after everyone was in bed; then we would quietly prepare the sleeping area for us in the living room. We spent most of our time at school and window-shopping in the evening so that we did not have to deal with all unpleasant moments at home.

The owner, the landlord of the property, was a kind man from Germany who came to the United States in the sixties. I approached him and told him of my dilemma. I asked him if I could move my family to the garage behind his house, which was only a block away. He said he did not mind the many of us living in his apartment, for he knew how hard it was for him when he first came to America to start his new life for his family. He was willing and happy to help me move into his garage, but I needed to take a look at it first before I made that decision.

It was a Sunday afternoon on a typical sunny day in California. I went over to his house to look at his garage, as he had asked me. He let me inside his house, through which we both walked to the back where the garage was located.

It was a twenty-by-forty-square-foot shed with a metal roof. Its three sides were walled with plywood, and the front of it was open. The whole place was packed full of all kinds of junk from auto parts to carpentry tools, from mattresses to used carpets, from broken beds to old TVs, to garden tools, all of which had been accumulated over the years. I was dumbfounded at the sight. It made me think and feel like it was the mouth of a monster being choked with stuff and its tongue was caught open and stuck. Karl, the name of my landlord, a carpenter by profession, had a tendency to bring home from work just about anything and everything that was being discarded at the jobsite, thinking that someday he would need it or use it. Obviously, the supply and demand was way off balance, as shown here in the garage.

The quick thought ran through my mind that it would take us weeks to empty his garage, and where on earth would I find space to put his stuff? As if reading my mind, he told me that I could put his things, his stuff, out in front of the garage and cover it with a sheet of tarp to protect it from the weather. I thanked him for his kindness and told him that I would think it over before I took on the project. In the meantime, my little family continued with its day-out-night-in schedule, until one day a tenant of his apartment next door who had not paid his rent and had been served with an eviction notice finally moved out. Karl asked me to move in. It was another happy day of my life when I physically moved into this three-bedroom house. The rent was a little more than what I could afford at the time, but I told Karl I would be out there working and take care of it as soon as money came in. He was kind enough to let my family in without having to put up a security deposit, which I did not have anyway. What a feeling to be living in your own place, moving freely from one room to another, going to the restroom as you wish or need. Karl came over to show us how to use the oven in the kitchen and washer and dryer in the laundry room. He also showed me how to use the vacuum cleaner on his aged, dark teal-colored shaggy carpet. He was a good-hearted man who was always there to help me and show me life in America, sort of an old-timer coaching a new one. He had a nice family of a wife, a son, and a daughter, all of whom came over to our place quite often, and we all became good friends.

Shortly after we moved in, the school season started. Lam and Tuan, our sons, were registered for their classes at Santa Rita Elementary School, where we met Mrs. Marilyn Arnett, the secretary of the school, who displayed a special loving care for us. She came to our place to help make the window curtains and the beds as a mother would for her children. She then later allowed Lam to stay at her place for the whole school year as if he were her own grandson. She would take him to school when she went to work and home with her when she came home. Our kids called her grandma, and I called her mom. She is one of the angels in my life.

One evening, Karl called me after dinner, saying that he would come right over to take me for a job interview at the place he was working. I had asked him earlier to find me a job or to tell me about any job he saw that might fit me. I told him I would love to come with him any time, and before we hung up, I felt so happy with the job opportunity and so moved at his kindness.

Minutes later, it was raining, cold, and dark outside. I gathered some of my personal papers such as letters of recommendation from the UN and US Embassy in the Philippines and said good-bye to my wife and my kids. I hopped into the front seat with him in his yellowish Toyota truck with a canopy in the back. While driving, he told me that the owner of the place, whom he was working for, was looking for a handyman to help with clean up at the construction site and also perhaps someone who could help his wife take care of a newborn baby. He thought that I might want to give it a try. I told him I would love to do anything to feed my family and to make sure that he would not have to throw me out into the street for not paying him rent. From the faint dim light in his cabin, he turned over to give me a smile, the one of his approval, as he knew that I was not joking. He was definitely in my shoes to feel the feelings of a refugee man, a displaced person, for he had been an immigrant himself many years before.

He stopped and parked his truck in front of a very large two-story building that was well-lit up with tons of lights. There were many cars parked along the driveway all the way to the street, giving me the impression that there must be a gathering or a crowd inside. Perhaps there was a party going on that Karl had forgotten to tell me about or something of that nature, I wondered. I gathered my papers and got out of the vehicle and quickly ran to the building to avoid getting wet from the rain. Karl came right next to me at the front door and rang the bell.

Once inside, I was introduced to the owners of the property, Pete and Ann Bjorklund, both of whom gave me a feeling of warmth and safety and love to be around. After looking at the letters of recommendation from the United Nations and hearing the story of my plight coming to the US, they told me that they were looking for someone to help around the house and most importantly, to start with, for someone to help Ann take care of the newborn, Peter Jr., who was just a few weeks old. Peter told me if I'd like to take the job as handyman and my wife wanted to help take care of the baby boy, my wife could start as early as the next day. Pete told me that he would start my wife and me at eight dollars an hour. I almost screamed with joy for his generosity. Mr. Peter Bjorklund told me about his wonderful time he had spent in Thailand working and that he had fallen in love with the Asian culture. That being said, I felt immediately the connectedness between us. I was then introduced to other guests who had drinks in their hands, chatting, laughing cheerfully in the midst of soft music. They all seemed to be having a good time. I had been so intense on the job interview with the Bjorklunds that I had forgotten about the gathering occasion of the night. I never asked about it, for I was just so happy about the job, so excited about my first employment in America that Ann and Pete had just given me.

My wife and I were back at the Bjorklunds the following morning, full of energy and enthusiasm. It was still early in the morning. The front lawn was still wet from the rain the night before. The air was sweetened with the after-rain fragrance. The squirrels were startled at our presence and ran away off to the trees. Ann was waiting for us at her place. I was not supposed to be working but was there to help my wife to make sure that she understood all instructions from Ann. Once we were inside the house, we met the young Peter, were shown the house, and were told what needed to be done and what to expect. I went back outside, looking for something to do while my wife was with Ann working inside. I kept myself busy. I cleaned the backyard. I hosed off the dirty patio and did other odd things. I just felt that I wanted to engage in my own undefined tasks to keep her house and her yard nice and clean without being asked.

At the end of the day, she said she was very happy with my wife, Tammy, and that she also appreciated what I had done for her. She asked me to keep track of the time I spent working so that she could pay me as well. I told her I just did it to keep myself busy without expecting compensation. But her voice had a tone of authority, and we were all happy.

A few days after helping Tammy and Ann at her place, I began my work at the Bjorklunds' building, where there was a full-time crew of carpenters, painters, and masonry workers. It was early in the morning. I could see now the large aged oak trees in front and back of the building, which I had not noticed the night I came for the interview. The sound of machinery in motion was in one corner of the building, the radio was playing music in the other, and the workers moved about in different directions, which gave aliveness to the place I was about to work. After introductions to those workers on the ground, Ken, in his late fifties, who was in charge of construction and remodeling, asked me to operate the cement mixer and to bring the mud to the second floor using the scaffold.

Ken showed me how to mix the cement in the mixer with the right amount of water needed to blend in to bring about the kind of mortar he wanted for the work upstairs. When the switch from the mixer was turned off and the barrel stopped moving, I told Ken that I could handle it myself and thanked him for his caring instruction. He was such a nice and kind man that I immediately liked him. Ken and I continued to work and help each other years after this job was done.

The wet mud was now transferred to the bucket; Ken pointed his finger upward, where a couple of workers who were standing on top of the scaffold were waiting for the mud to work on their job.

"I want you to bring this up there and give it to the guys and make more as they need it," Ken told me. "And be careful when you walk on the planks," he added.

With the heavy bucket of mud in my hand, I climbed on the wooden planks of the wobbly scaffold, with its squeaky sound at each step I took, level after level, almost to the top. I was now in complete understanding the meaning of when he had said, "Be careful." Just one mistake, as I nervously looked down, off with my balance, I could be down there mingled with my mud, and holy cow! Things would be ugly. I was not acrophobic, but after many years of not climbing, things had changed. I had forgotten the climbing experiences of my childhood at the village where I would be on top of a fruit tree, out on the limbs of a branch to pick fruits for friends. In those old days, climbing was not a challenge, but it was more fun and adventure.

After the first and second batches of mud, up and down a few times, I got used to it and did it so well that I gained the trust and friendship of all the workers.

At lunch break, we were together in the backyard by the swimming pool. Since I was a new guy in the group and was a Vietnamese and a refugee, I was the target for many questions about life in Vietnam, the infamous war, and about my escape becoming one of the boat people. I told them what I knew and answered their questions to the best of my knowledge, unbiased. There was an incident during this lunch break that made me feel a little embarrassed, but it is worth remembering and mentioning. Tom D., a nice and experienced carpenter who really showed his caring for me, was sitting next to me by the edge of the pool. I was kind of admiring a gadget that was moving slowly at the bottom of the pool, wiggled by a water hose, like a water snake pushing this light blue gadget from one direction to another. The pool was full of clear water now reflected with the blue-colored wall of the pool. I noticed that this gadget had a sort of a net or a bag behind it, collecting leaves and debris. It dawned on me that it was a cleaner for the pool; it sucked up the leaves or any small debris at the bottom of the pool. As I was in awe and amazed at the gadget, in an exclamatory tone of voice, I said, "What a sucker!"

It caused attention as Tom and everyone else looked at me and laughed at my not-too-appropriate expression, but they understood what I meant. The day went by quickly, and I came home physically exhausted. After dinner, I went right to bed and slept like baby.

I continued to work at the Bjorklunds, cleaning up after the workers and doing handyman's work, keeping the front and backyards clean and the grass mowed and fertilized. I also signed up for classes at the Foothill Community College as a full-time student thanks to the flexible schedule at work. In addition, I landed a part-time job in the evening at the El Camino Hospital in Mountain View. It all started in my English class, in which Shirley, my classmate who sat next to me, asked me if I would like to work in the food service department, where she was a supervisor. She told me that if I wanted, I could come to her department the following day to see her department director. It was how it all got started. I went to see her and her boss the following day. Joan Davis, a cheerful lady, was head of the food service department and gave me a job as dishwasher. She wanted to start me as soon as my physical exams were complete. It was scheduled to be done at the hospital as well.

The two part-time jobs and twelve- to fourteen-credit work-load at school kept me on my toes. My weekend schedule was filled either with work at the hospital or odd jobs from yard cleaning to hauling unwanted items to the public dump from private parties. Money was always out there to be made, and I wanted to take advantage of all opportunities to financially support my folks back home and enjoy the education being offered at the college.

My first car in the US was a Ford 1970 Maverick I bought for one thousand dollars from a friend at school. It had lot of miles on its record, but it did have a rebuilt engine and an aged look of light teal blue. I did not have much of a choice. I did what I could from what I had saved from many working days. After all, it was a vehicle that I owned outright without financing; it was a very dependable car, and we all in my family were proud to have it. I was now able to take my boys to school, to church, and do oriental grocery shopping, which was about half an hour away in downtown of San Jose. Most importantly of all, I could go to school plus go to work with it on time. I enjoyed driving it until the day our cousin Le Nguyen arrived from Chicago. I gave it to him so that he could get around, and after that, he let his friend have it too.

A year had gone by quickly. I was able to reconnect with Dr. Tim Vo and other friends from the refugee camp in Palawan. Tim was living in New York, and others were scattered all over the country from Virginia to Texas to Los Angeles. I asked Dr. Vo if he would consider moving to California to stay with us; he said he needed a little time to sleep on that thought and would eventually let me know.

FIRST HOME

Because I had been able to work and had a steady income, even at a small scale, we started talking about having a house of our own. Through some friends in the community, a realtor was recommended, and the search for the house began. I was a bit apprehensive at first due to the limited income coming in from both of our jobs, but the idea of renting some of the room space out to help with mortgage payment eased my concerns, and the decision was then made to go with the purchase. At this point in time, we did not know anything about credit rating or credit qualification for mortgage financing. All we were told by the realtor was that he would take care of us and that all we needed to worry about was a down payment and the rest would take care of itself. The talk sounded easy and convincing to the extent that we let the realtor handle all the transactions and paperwork. Part of it was trust, and the rest was ignorance.

After seeing a few houses, we narrowed our search to a house on Socorro Avenue in Sunnyvale. It was in a rather quiet neighborhood, not too far from work, and the entrance to freeways was a couple of minutes away. The school for the boys was only in walking distance.

It was a three-bedroom, two-bath standard house without a basement. It had an average-sized backyard for a garden. The whole lot was all fenced in with wooden fence. The house was characterized with two large-sized broad-leaf trees at the front of the house, which were excellent for shade. These favorable elements along with an asking price of $97,000 seemed a fair deal. Now the dilemma was that we were short of cash for the $5,000 down payment plus closing costs. We had no friends, no relatives to borrow from, and no other resources to turn to. Then came a creative idea from the agent: bump the sale price up by the difference, the seller will refund it, then the question of money for the down payment and closing cost was no longer a concern. I thought it was just a brilliant creative idea and solution, except that because I was just ignorant, I did not know the complexity of the banking system that was involved in the purchase of real estate. This brought me lots of headaches in later years.

When we moved into the house, only then when all papers were given to us did we find out that none of the documents had our names on them. We were then told that all would be transferred to our names later, perhaps in a few months, and the agent would personally take care of it for us. In the meantime, it bore the names of a couple that we had just become acquainted with, and they would give a deed of trust to us in a month or so at the county of Santa Clara. The bank, according to the agent, would follow with the transfer to our names. Two years later, when the interest rate dropped down from 21 percent to 11 percent and we discovered there was a five-year balloon payment, which we were not informed of, I called the agent about the promise he had made. His answer was that it was too late and he could no longer help. Disappointed at this, I called up the bank to which I had been making monthly payments and asked if our names could be put on the loan instead. Fortunately, the payments had been made with our checks from our personal checking account, and the banker was happy to help us. The fee was only fifty dollars, he said, and all was done. I also asked the bank to refinance the high interest rate loan to the current one of 11 APR. This was a learning lesson for me.

What a feeling to own your very own house! All of us were very happy to live in a house in which we enjoyed our freedom to alternate, to change, and to grow our own garden. First things first, we had to haul away a pile of junk at the side and back of the house so that a garden could be cultivated with some colors of ethnic vegetables. Then came the conversion of the garage into a living space for Dr. Vo, who was spending his time studying for his medical exams to validate his medical license in the US. He quietly passed the exams and made no big deal about his accomplishment. We also began to draw in some friends, first one and then two from the Palawan camp, who all helped and chipped in to make our monthly mortgage payment less burdensome. This did not come easily. There were some compromises, some inconveniences in this little community of friends and friends of friends, but we managed to get through the difficult times and moved on.

The holidays in America were approaching faster than I was prepared for. Ann and Pete, our employers and friends, had been so wonderfully kind to all of us. They made sure that we were all cared and provided for, and in return, we wanted to match theirs with our love and dedication to take care of their family as our own. Nhan, our sister, was now living with them after an incident in which she was harassed on her school bus coming home from school. She was crying all the way to our house, and after hearing the story the following day, Pete and Ann asked to have her stay with them so she could go to her school in their area. Ann would take her to school and pick her up and care for as one of her own. After her high school years, Nhan was then sent to private school of fashion at their expense. Pete and Ann have now adopted her to become their daughter, and now she is called Nan.

Ann was the first one to give us the taste of turkey for Thanksgiving, and she showed us everything else about the celebration. We were definitely the ones who had a lot to be thankful for. The air and the spirit of this holiday brought us to the solemn realization of the true meaning of Thanksgiving. Besides our plight, our yearlong journey from the other side of the planet, we were placed in the hands of angels who eased our pain and guided us every day to a brighter future. They were the ones who gingerly helped us into the new culture, the tradition of sharing and giving during the holiday seasons. Tammy and I helped Ann sort out gifts and wrap and label them. This started right after Thanksgiving, and it would take days into December to complete this task. I remember someone said: "Walking by the federal treasury building, I feel generous." I now surely felt the generosity by being around Ann and Pete. Their Christmas presents to us were not only plentiful in physical material terms, but also more than anything else, were their hearts of caring and helping. From this I learned the art of giving and the profound meaning of receiving. As Shakespeare says in his wonderful lines of poetry called "Mercy," "It droppeth as the gentle rain from heaven, upon the place beneath; it is twice blest. It blesseth him that gives, and him that takes."

Ann and Pete were not just raindrops of blessing from heaven. Monsoons of kindness from their hearts soaked every one of us in loving care. For example, a dishwasher, a portable one given to us as a Christmas present from Ann and Pete, made my coworkers jealous. During our break at the food service department, where I worked as a part-time diswasher, I told my fellow workers about Ann and Pete, about the gifts, and how I came to know and to work for them. They said that they wished they had someone like Pete and Ann to work for. I guess we were all fortunate to be drawn to them so that they could put us under their wing, and we were never the same. Their love and kindness were just so contagious that I would like to be like them someday.

I remember an incident in which we were asked to take a vacation; it was in the summertime and our first vacation in the US. They handed me the keys to their Suburban, a map to their vacation house in the mountains in Mendocino County, a rifle, and a shotgun to keep all of us safe from bears and other animals. I was deeply moved at this, thinking how many employers out there would have this kind of treatment toward their employees and their families. I doubted there were any.

This very first summer vacation for our family in the United States changed my life in such a way that I would never have thought possible. After we had everything loaded into the Suburban, from rice to bagged noodles and other food and drinks to Chinese martial arts movies, all good for one week's entertainment and nourishment, we took off heading to the mountains. After hours of driving, following the directions, we finally arrived at the gate to the mountain house, which was located way up almost to the top of the mountain. It was isolated, and I could see no other houses around as I drove on the dirt road leading to the house. It was still early in the afternoon on a warm sunny day, and it was so very quiet as we got to the house. I parked the truck underneath the shade of the tree next to the house so that we could unload our belongings and slide them into the house through the side door. In front of the house, a three-bedroom, one bath, fully furnished, was a round pond about the size of the large swimming pool, half-full of water. Flowers in colors were blooming along the edges of the pond, and the dragonflies found their haven at this seemingly only spot with water in this mountainous region. Frogs made their jumps into the water as they were startled at the discovery of invaders in their territory.

The whole area seemed to be absorbed into the heat and the quietness of the summer day. It felt like the upper nineties or even a hundred degrees. A few birds chirping on top of the tree next to the house drew my attention. Out of the blue, out of my curiosity about the two rifles Pete had handed me earlier for our protection, I got to the truck and pulled out the single-shot rifle, which was well hidden under the seat of the vehicle. I thought to myself that I had not used guns or fired a rifle for many years, and I wanted to give it a try to see if I was still a good shooter, or in this case, a hit-not-miss sniper. I loaded a single round of bullets into the gun. All of my troops had gone inside the house, where it was cooler. I was all by myself with a desire to aim at something, to pull the trigger, to find out how good I still was at shooting. The chirping of the birds, the flopping of their wings from one branch to another, caused me to look up, and so I aimed at a little bird that perched on a branch high above. I slowly pulled the trigger and *pow!* The jerk of the barrel, the smoke and the smell of the gunpowder, and the falling of a little bird that dropped onto the ground all seemed to happen at the same time. I bent down to pick up the bird and saw a few drops of blood hanging on the ruffled, battered feathers of the motionless bird, and at that moment, I was transformed. A feeling of guilt and remorse ate at me, and I was forever changed. No more killings, no more shootings, I told myself, from that moment on.

Right after an early dinner, we were all glued to the screen to watch the Chinese kung fu martial arts movies that we had rented at downtown San Jose for the trip. We stayed up the first night through the second night until the following morning. It was almost forty hours before we decided to take a break to catch up with our sleep, and besides, the video player had overheated! Ramen noodles were the only food we used during the thirty-six hours of home entertainment. We had consumed the whole case. It was convenient and easy to fix, and we all had good time feeling as if we were camping. The following days were very relaxing. My boys and I went out into the woods to explore the area surrounding the house. The bears had actually come to our place and made a mess at the garbage area. However, I had lost interest in using guns even just as a method of chasing them away.

Our employment with Ann and Pete had entered into the third year; we had become more like family than the employees and employers. Little Peter was now three years old and had been well-cared for by two mothers, Mommy Tam and Mommy Ann. In fact, our closeness earned Tam her title "Mommy Tam" and me "Uncle Sam." We would normally come to watch the house for days when Ann and Pete needed to be out of town on business or on their getaway for a few days. On these occasions, more often than not, we were asked to bring home some bottles of milk, which were delivered from the local dairy to Ann's place twice a week. As these glass bottles of milk got home, which were distinguishable from the ones bought at the grocery store, we would call it "Mommy Ann's milk." It was said in such a way that at first, it was just a differentiating expression, but immediately after chuckles from adult guys in my household, it became amusing, and it went on for years.

Along with all the blessings from the Arnetts and the Bjorklunds came the news that we were going to have a baby. Tammy's pregnancy after twelve years from our last child brought a joyful surprise to all relatives and friends alike. Mommy Ann was asked to pick the name for our baby, and she was absolutely delighted to take on the task. We decided to enjoy the patience of waiting, counting the days to pass by, and most of all, to look forward to having a surprise—a boy or a girl was the entire blessing.

On the twenty-fifth of February 1984, on the second floor at El Camino Hospital where I worked, my baby boy was born. I was blessed to be in the labor room and saw him delivered. Out of the three children, this was the only one that I had the privilege to be with my wife and to hear the first cry of my boy. At that critical moment, the delivering doctor asked my wife to give another push. Tammy, tempted to heed the advice but almost out of breath, in her exhaustion, said, "I can't," but with her last strength, she gave one last push, and my boy greeted the world with his cry. After seeing all of this, I now fully understood the meaning of *labor* for a woman delivering her babies. It was a matter of life with joy and celebration, but there was also a possibility of death as well. At this moment I caught a glimpse of the miracle of life itself. The delivering physician, Dr. Weber, then turned to me after removing his surgical gloves from his hands. "Congratulations, Mr. Le! You have a beautiful and healthy boy here," he said.

I showed him my deep gratitude and uttered my very sincere thanks to him for all of his loving care and hard work. The best of all was his professionalism to usher my child into the world. I told him my son's name as he asked.

The name was Jonathan. Mommy Ann picked the name for him, and we all loved it. During the two days at the hospital, I was advised that the circumcision should be performed, which was a bit of decision to be made by the father, who had never had it, and neither did all other boys in the family. After all, it was not very popular in our tradition. I was, however, inclined to the idea and its benefits and okayed the procedure. As soon as we got all the instructions from the staffing nurses on the caring for the baby, we had him home at last.

All our relatives and friends were happy on the birth of my child. Dr. Tim Vo proudly and happily came in to play the role of godfather. He accepted our request with enthusiasm, and he has been the best godfather I've ever known. He held my child and carried the lit candle on his hand at the baptismal ceremony at the Lady of Lourdes Catholic Church in Sunnyvale. The transformation from symbolism of caring and guidance into the actuality of full support materially and spiritually has continued until today.

Jonathan continued to grow and was a happy boy. We now would take him to work at Ann's every day, and we all took turns caring for him. Mommy Ann was so fond of him as if he were her own child. She would feed him, bathe him, change his diapers, and do much more as a loving, caring mother would. Ann and Pete loved my kids as their own. Even though Lam and Tuan now have families of their own, presents still come to them on their birthdays and Christmastime. Kids in my family do treasure Ann as their second mother.

Now came the better-than-good news from Ann and Pete that Ann was pregnant. It seemed as if Ann and Tammy were in competition for babies, and we all were very thrilled at the news.

Ashley Bjorklund arrived, bringing with her all the health and charm a beautiful baby girl could bring. Now that her brother, Peter Jr., was old enough, all attention was shifted to her. I myself even had chances to care for her from diaper changing to bathing and feeding her. The sense of loving and caring for one another was always felt at Ann and Pete's place.

I continued to spend my time at the Bjorklunds, hospital, and at school. Tammy's girlfriend Hao, a classmate from high school years, came to stay with us. One day at the flea market in San Jose, we found out that the silk floral booth was always busy with happy faces of customers. This prompted us to take a closer look at possibilities of having a floral business for her. After checking and learning and buying inventories for the business, we went to a weekend event at the De Anza Community College campus flea market. It was a lot of work for the three of us, and the next thing we knew, our friend could not handle the work, which required lots of time for preparation, especially getting up early in the morning. She threw in the towel, and we ended up doing it ourselves.

Weekend after weekend, month after month, we would haul our floral products to sell at this flea market. We had purchased a used box van to keep our supplies and inventories in it all the time so that we did not have to spend a lot of time loading and unloading the merchandise into the house when the day was over at the market. We would have all of our kids come to help with the business; one would make the floral arrangements, another did the selling and customer service, and another was cashier.

I made the trees, mostly ficus, palm, and aralias, during the week, especially at night after coming home from work at the hospital. They were now on the ground, standing up in the morning sun along with hanging baskets of fuchsias, petunias, geraniums, and other colorful flowers that made our booth a spectacular spot that drew lots of customers; and the business was good, considering it was just a part-time or weekend job. The word got out at the hospital that the trees I made looked very realistic, and as a result, orders started coming in at the rate I had to work harder, day and night, to fill all the orders. If this business of artificial trees and flowers was this good in this part of California, where real fresh plants and flowers and trees were ample and fresh all the time, I then wondered if I could start a business for ourselves somewhere else where the weather was different, where the weather allowed only white snow on the ground in the wintertime and bare trees in the autumn.

Spokane, Washington, was a place mentioned in a conversation between Tammy and Kim Nham, her girlfriend from high school in Vietnam. Kim Nham and her family had been living in the Spokane area for quite some time and wanted to move to

California for a change. One day her husband and his brother came to my house for a visit and inquired about job opportunities in my area so that they could move out of Spokane. I immediately called my food service department at the hospital and spoke with my department director, Joan Davis, about the possibility of hiring them to work in the dish room. She said, "Mr. Le, with your recommendation, I would love to have them in the dish room." I gave both of them my advice and assessment of the cost of living in the bay area from rent to other basic essential living expenses to make sure that it was a right move for them. I also asked them to take us to their home to look at the artificial flower market in the Spokane area. If the business opportunity was viable, if they both wished, we would form a floral business, and they would be a part of the corporation.

The following day we took off for Spokane. It was a long drive of more than thirteen hours on the road. It was not easy because our $300 1978 Ford Econoline van started showing signs of problems. It was burning oil like a chimney, which we had not been aware of before the trip. We had to stop every once in a while to put more oil into the engine to keep it going. The good thing was that it did not breakdown on the road. We finally arrived at the city of Spokane; the name means "children of the sun" in the local Indian tribal language. After getting some rest, we started looking at the Yellow Pages in the local phone book to locate all the floral shops in the Spokane area. We wanted to visit all of them to see what they had to offer.

Out on the road on the mission, after seeing a few floral shops, we felt that we would do well here. There were no silk flower shops in the area. We found a few shops that carried some silk floral, but they mixed with the fresh stems. They did not offer the selections and quality of the products that were available to us in California. With this insight, we felt that we could start our artificial floral business in this city, where the population was the second largest, only next to Seattle of Washington State. While doing the business survey, we also discovered that life in this city was somehow at a lot slower pace than that in

California. Everyone seemed to take time to smile to say hello to greet a passerby, and there was a kindness and genuineness in their expressions.

It was late in the afternoon; I was sitting in the car while my party was grocery shopping. Jonathan was having a late nap, and the window was about two-thirds down to let the cool air in. I was in shock when people walked by, waving at me. They smiled at me, and they would greet me, "How are you?" or "How are you doing?"

This type of interaction did not even exist in any public parking lots where I lived. I was very impressed at the friendliness of the people there. It was so impressive that, through our friends, the Vietnamese people who lived there, we learned that their children were doing well in school and were able to complete their education even at prestigious private colleges in the area such as Gonzaga University and Whitworth College. This information was more important and encouraging to me than anything else. I had risked and devoted my life to bringing up my children, and I intended to give them the best and have them as educated as they could be.

Prior to this trip to Spokane, there had been a few incidents in which Tuan, a junior in high school, would call home from a public phone at a shopping mall to let me know that he was hanging out with his friends and that he would come home later. That worried me, and I began to see the similar patterns of those children who had become gang members. At the beginning, they hung out with a wrong crowd, were influenced by them, and were gradually distanced from the family and were lost to the uncontrollable world of drugs and gangs. I could not and would not let it happen to my kids at any cost. Our decision to move to Spokane was made while I was driving home after weighing all elements of pros and cons. Education for our children was all we would strive for and was the highest priority of our lives.

OFF TO THE GREAT
NORTHWEST

Three weeks later, it was July 17, 1987, seven years after arriving in the United States of America; we were packed and rolled in our old beaten-up van (engine just now rebuilt after the first trip) to Spokane with a determination of raising our children and building a business of our own.

At the hospital, I had secured a verbal agreement from Mr. Brown, head of the medical records department, where I had been transferred after my graduation from Foothill College a year earlier. The agreement was that I could come back to my same job, same position and same pay rate, after one year if I decided to come back. Mr. Brown told me that he had presented my request to the administration and that they had never had granted such a petition, but it was approved on his behalf.

It was the hardest thing to for us to talk to Ann and Pete about our wanting to move away from them and do a business of our own even at the embryo stage. The family tie between us was so strong that breaking away from them was just as painful as it was to leave my homeland in my escape years before. The only difference was that I'd still call, I'd still come and visit. Still, it was not easy. Pete told me, even though he knew in his heart that there was something more than just the money that I was longing for, that he could give us good salary raises if we would stay. Finally, seeing our determination and the chance for us to be where we wanted to be, Ann and Pete told us that if for any reason ever needed to come back, their door was always wide open for us. Their arms would always be ready to embrace us, and they were always there to help if we ever needed them.

They must have known that it was not going to be easy to start a business in a new environment. "Where is Spokane?" my friends would curiously ask me, and even my kids would challenge our choice of moving to this locality, for it was not a place they ever heard of; therefore, it was not a popular place to live. Tuan asked me, "Why Spokane out of many other places? Besides, I have all of my friends here. I don't want to go," he would protest. But a year or so later, they all said we had made a right choice.

The summer in Spokane was winding down. We had been using Kim's garage to display our products and placed signs at corners of the streets in the neighborhood to draw in customers. A few customers had come; some made a purchase, and some gave compliments to our products without buying. But most of all, the enthusiastic reception of artificial botanicals in this small community was quite encouraging for us. And we made some money even on the very tiny scale of operating business.

Realizing that we had to move out of Kim's place so that their garage could be utilized for housing their cars when winter came, we decided to buy a house at a location that could offer accessibility and a good amount of traffic as well.

Through a realtor's help, we settled on a property on University Road in the valley of Spokane, which had ample space at the front of the house plus a semicircle driveway that would allow customers to come in and out without any difficulty. There was very large backyard that we practically used as a soccer field, and as a bonus, a swimming pool was right at the back door. All of us swam every day until the weather turned cold at the end of September.

After we moved in, we immediately turned the garage into a little floral shop with a new coat of paint, put shelving against the walls, and used a small table for a calculator. All of these were created and accomplished within the first week of our moving in. We also obtained a business license for our operations. A couple of folding signs were created and placed at the corners of the street. The colorful hanging baskets of fuchsias and geraniums on the rack in front of the building were the only marketing tools we had to bring customers in.

With the very little experience and knowledge of running a business acquired at the flea market previously, we now applied it to the actual business setting that there was so much still to learn, and we learned every day from customers. We asked questions and listened to the customers and stayed focused on making sure that those who came to purchase or even just to pay a visit were happy when they left, and we always asked them for referrals. From the first day of our business in our garage, people started to come in to patronize, and gradually, day after day, more and more from the community came to visit us. We were very pleased and felt blessed at the support that the community had given us, a new kid on the block.

When fall came, our flower hanging baskets still showed bright and cheerful while the leaves on the maple trees at the corners of our house and elsewhere on the street had turned colors and left their branches. These perceived permanent colorful flowers at this time of the year had created curiosity from the passersby, and as a result, the cash register kept ringing and customers kept coming all the way through the winter.

We had approached Kim's husband and her brother-in-law to talk about forming a partnership in business so that we could go into a commercial location when spring came. But they were all reluctant to take us up on the offer because there was always an element of uncertainty in the business, especially a new one like ours, as opposed to the biweekly paychecks they were enjoying. We did not want to push them into the situation in which no one knew for sure if the paychecks were sure things for everyone. Most importantly, we did not want to ruin our friendship.

The period of testing the water was over; we felt that if the business was this good in this residential location, it would definitely be better in a commercial location. At this time, I had been hired as a social worker for the Department of Health and Services to serve the refugee community in the Spokane area. I took the job as a security cushion for the family, even though I knew that it was going to be hard on Tammy, who was going to work all by herself including taking Jonathan to school in the morning and picking him up in the afternoon. But we all managed to get by as we used to in the past. We had made up our mind to do this business and raise our family in this friendly environment, and we were going to focus on making it happen.

To run a business in a garage, which is wide open in the wintertime, was not an easy job. It was so cold that none of us could be outside in the garage for a long period of time. We only came out when someone appeared at the driveway and quickly went inside after the customer was gone. The summertime, which quickly slipped by, was not favorable either. When it reached ninety-nine and higher outside, it would feel like being inside an oven and would surely make one sweat.

For the first time in my life, I signed a commercial lease for a building on Division Street, which was one of the two main roads that divided Spokane into east and west. The building had 3,500 square feet on the main floor and an upstairs of equivalent retail space. The basement was quite spacious and just perfect for merchandise inventory storage. A local merchant friend who had been doing business in Spokane for quite some time and seemed knowledgeable on the subject of commercial locations recommended this location. The lease required lots of personal information and credit ratings, all of which were not a problem. However, since I had no history of renting a commercial building, I was asked to have a credible cosigner. Well, I was thinking of asking Ann and Pete, who might not mind doing it for me, but on the other hand, I did not want to bother anyone or become a burden or liability. Instead, I went directly to the agent and explained my situation. I was a newcomer trying to build a new life in America. I told him that I did not have any rental history with commercial real estates, but I did have on the residential. On top of that, I had all the references he needed, including the letters from the United Nations. He was kind enough and agreed to let us in. Like a professional negotiator, I asked for three months of free rent for remodeling and sprucing up the inside to make it look like a decent floral shop. Surprisingly, he said that he would talk to the landlord and it should not be a problem. The lease was finally signed for five years with an option for an additional five years with a 3 percent increase each year.

I turned in my two-week notice to my supervisor simultaneously with the signing of my lease for my store because I knew that it would require more than my full-time commitment to make it a success. Henry, my department supervisor, who did not want me to leave, had a word of advice for me that doing business, especially in a business of fake flowers, was very risky and that I should not leave this job, which provided a good steady income and most of all, job security with the DSHS. I knew he meant well and very much appreciated his good heart and kindness. I told him that I always wanted to do something on my own and that was why I left my very secure jobs in California to come to Spokane to start my own business. I knew it was risky and definitely not easy. But how would I know the taste of success or failure if I did not try? I also told him that if worse came to worst, I would consider myself as if I had just gotten off the boat and start all over again and again if I had to. A year later after my store opened, Henry stopped in at the store, which was well decorated and fully displayed with merchandise. He said, "My hat is off to you, Mr. Le; you have made it. I wished I had the guts to do what I wanted to do."

I told him that it is never too late to do what one really wants to do. During my time with him, or working for him, we shared the talk of our cultures, his from Mexico and mine from Vietnam. He had recipes, or his grandma's secrets, of making tortillas and dipping sauce, which, according to him, "will knock your socks off," but it never left the stage of ideas. It was never translated into action.

With the help from two fellow Vietnamese, a father and a son, whom we had met at the flea market in San Jose earlier, we were able to get the store open in time for business.

On the grand opening day, despite all the many laborious hours to get things ready from making products to preparing the floor to cleaning up the mess left by the sign makings, counter trimmings, and nameless other things, we had only a quarter of the store space displayed with merchandise for sale. We had worked very hard every day and every night paneling the walls, painting inside and outside the building. We did everything by ourselves except for the minor electrical modification to the wiring to fit into our designs and the new carpet installation on the main floor. The night before the grand opening day, we did not leave the building until four o'clock in the morning. As we were exiting the building through the front door to go home to get ourselves cleaned up for the big day, I noticed the faint pink color of light at the horizon far away. It was the light of a new day to begin, and I realized that we had not slept for almost forty hours, but the excitement of grand opening just kept us going and going.

It was a good grand opening day, considering we had not done any advertising for the event and that the floor had a large empty space without merchandise. But it was a rewarding day for all of us hardworking people. For days and months to come, we continued to enjoy the growth of our business.

The success of the business also brought along the jealousy and greed from the two helpers whom we had trusted and treated like members of our family. Unfortunately, they had conspired with some other individuals in town to create the same type of business in the downtown area. They began to gradually take our inventories from our basement to their place. This was done initially at the end of the working hours when the stolen merchandise was placed inside the garbage dumpster and taken home when they left the building. But later on, it was done at the midnight hours, as his friend in San Jose who knew what was happening told me. This person was their friend who came to

Spokane at one time for a visit while we were all working on the inside of the building. He called me and told me of their conspiracy, their stealing scheme, and their schedule of taking out the stock. He wanted to call to let me know what was going on but did not want to see them in jail. If he had, I would not have had any hesitation to put them behind the bars.

These crooks disappeared and never returned. I later discovered that their disappearance was a result of the involvement of FBI agents who were looking for them. I did not know the reason for the FBI's interest. It happened as if there were some sort of invisible divine protection of us from these men's ill intentions. We had been somewhat worried that they might harm us while we knew nothing of their whereabouts. We had been living in a state of alert and taking precautious actions wherever we went until we heard that the FBI was looking for them. We continued with the business and were doing well. We seemed to have introduced the right products at the right time, as some of our friends would comment on our success.

Twelve years had gone by; the lease on this building was up for renewal, but the new lease was going to be almost double in rent. It was a very tough call. I thought that this was some sort of a bluff from the landlord, who knew that I had had a good, solid business on this location and that I would not want to move out. Yes, he was right; I did not want to, but on the other hand, I did not want to give him all of my profit in rent. I knew that he would do it again and again as long as I was his tenant and he my landlord.

With that in mind, we were determined that we would become our own landlords. I took my book to the bank where I was doing my banking on a daily basis and asked for help. A US bank official, after reviewing my financial performance, told me that half a million dollars was available for me to either fund a new construction project or to purchase an existing building. It was just a good feeling that the possibility of owning a commercial building and becoming my own landlord was just a matter of locating the right location to move the business to.

Miracles do happen, and in my lifetime, I have experienced and seen miracles many a times. Here is a classic example, the purchase of my very first commercial building ever since I came to the US.

It began one evening when, after closing the store, my wife and I had to drive to deliver a floral arrangement to a customer in the South Hill area. It was a special order, and the instruction was to have the arrangement delivered late in the evening after work. Upon arrival at the address, it was a business place, and the recipient, a middle-aged man, was waiting in his office for his order. While he was complimenting the floral arrangement that the colors perfectly matched the decor of his office and he praised my talented wife for her skills of designs, I cast my eyes up the wall above his desk and caught sight of some of sizable plaques hung on the wall, all of which showed recognition of him as a builder and contractor. Then, after confirming that he was, I poured out my dilemma of being in a situation in which my rent was going to be doubled and that I was looking for a build-ing to buy or perhaps, construct a new building. He said that he would be very happy to help me build one that suited my needs. However, he said, "There is a sizable building on Ruby Street at the Foothill that I believe is for sale. You might want to check it out."

We left his office after saying a big thank you to him and also getting his business information. We promised that we would to stay in touch.

The next morning, I asked my realtor friend, Greg Byrd, to find out who owned that building and all the information per-taining to that piece of property.

"The Department of Transportation, the DOT, owns it," he said to me over the phone the following day. After spending some time gathering the information, he gave me the phone number to call for details.

I talked with Michelle, the DOT representative for the Spokane office, who was genuinely cheerful over the phone and told me that she would meet us at the building to give us a tour.

She also said that she would be available to show the building if I could come over right away. Minutes later, we were at the building, which I had driven by hundreds of times over the course of the past years but had never paid any attention to. It was boarded up with particleboard at the facade of the building, and its front and entrance were littered with all kinds of trash, discarded signs, and mounds of dirt now covered with half-dying grass. Empty bottles, cans, and plastic bags scattered at every turn gave me a feeling that it was just a run-down building and no one wanted it. *That was probably why it has been sitting here for such a long time,* I thought.

As we were let inside the building, I immediately noticed some parts of the ceiling where Sheetrock and other insulation materials were dangling and about to fall down on our heads, and other parts of the spacious floor were piled up with drywall and building materials. There was a decaying odor in the air inside the building that was hard to pinpoint. It could very well be from the rotten part of the ceiling that was affected by the leaky roof, or it could be from mold, or the combination of all of them. It gave me a feeling that the building had not been cared for and it had not been occupied for a very long time. As a matter-of-fact, it needed major repairs. I wondered if I could financially afford the task of overhauling it, bringing it to where it should be for a retail business.

I uttered that concern to Tammy, and her response was, "I like the location." Indeed, the building was situated on an isolated, sizable lot curving toward the main street of Spokane. The building was now just half of the original size when the DOT purchased in order to complete the construction of north and southbound lanes of Division Street. It was visible to both directions of traffic, especially the northbound traffic. One could go straight into the building if one did not curve in the road.

After learning the recent history of the building and its asking price, I, as if buying a car at the used-car lot, asked Michelle how much the monthly payment would be if one could purchase it. Pulling out her chestnut brown-colored Hewlett Packer hand-held computer, moving her fingers over number keys, she gave me a number that was just about $180 more than my current monthly rent, provided I won the bid, she emphasized. She went on to explain the practice of the DOT selling their real estate properties. They went through a sealed-bid process in which a minimum dollar amount was given, in this case, $525,000, one hundred thousand less from the previous minimum asking price. With all excitement and enthusiasm, I began to ask her about the time the bidding process was going to be held and all other pertinent information on the bidding process. I could see that my chance of owning a piece of commercial land was so close, so real, that I asked her how many people, how many realtors had looked into this building and how many had she shown herself. She said, "Quite a few, but you have shown the most interest in it." I told her about my situation with the rent being increased and that I must make my move to get out of where I was and most importantly, that here was a chance for me to have a place of my own.

Leaving the building after a brief survey of the outside and inside of the building, we went home with mixed feelings, excited about the opportunity at hand, but nervous about the chances of getting it. As Michelle mentioned, there had been other people showing interest in the building. They were high-profile real estate investors in this town, and the chance for me to outbid them was slim to none.

The following days were filled with phone calls and visits to Michelle's office to learn of the process of sending in the bid. Knowing that I really wanted to win the bid or to be able to purchase the building, she could not give any advice other than to make sure that I followed the procedures correctly, to make sure the forms were properly filled out, and to make sure that I gave it plenty of time to get there.

The day that I mailed out the deposit, a cashier's check, to Olympia, where the auction was going to take place, I informed Michelle about the mailing and asked her if she knew anyone who would let her know the result of the bidding and if I ever was a winner, to please let me know right away. She looked at me with her usual kindness and said, "Since you really want the building and are so persistent, I will do it for you."

I have never been a gambler in my life for money, but I may have done that in this case. I filled out the bidding forms with lots of thought and calculation. First, I thought I would never be able to match any real estate guys in this town in terms of finance and expertise, and because of that thinking, I figured that any amount larger than the minimum that I could afford would be unmatchable by theirs. Second, I went ahead and added ten dollars to the minimum-bid amount along with my silent prayers, comforting myself that if it was to be mine, then it would be mine. This was done quietly between the divine and me, and me only.

Days went by, and I was anxiously waiting for the result; I was counting down each day to that moment. Lam had gone to Paris with his buddy to watch the World Cup soccer games and was anxious as well. He called me the day before D-day, thinking that it was the day of opening the sealed bids, to see if I had been the winner. I told him that he was in a different time zone and that he should just enjoy watching the game, for that was the whole purpose of going to France. Nevertheless, I told him that I would not expect to have the news of the results for a couple of days and I would save the good news for him.

Early in the afternoon following the D-day, the phone rang. "Is this Mr. Le?"

I said yes as I answered the phone. It was Michelle's voice that I had been anxiously waiting for. I felt my heart pounding faster as if my whole being was rushing for the news.

"Are you sitting down? I have news for you."

There was a little playfulness in her voice, prolonging the dramatic moment of her delivery of the news.

"Yes," again I said to her. "Please tell me the good news."

She said, "You have it! The building is yours!"

Her voice softened with kindness. I screamed out loud with so much joy and excitement and said thank you to her.

"You won the bid, and congratulations, Mr. Le. Come to see me in a day or two to work on the papers."

It turned out that the DOT offered to finance the building for me at a very competitive rate with no loan fees. That alone saved me a lot of money, at least five thousand dollars.

I felt the divine touch in the whole thing of acquiring of this building. Everyone I came into contact with concerning this property seemed to have been lined up by invisible divine intelligence to help and guide me each step from the beginning to the end—the contractor, who, instead of making money on building my place, offered me information to look into this building; Greg Byrd, the realtor friend, who checked and provided information leading to Michelle, the DOT representative, who showed kindness and patience to help me in the process. These individuals, who are angels in disguise, came to aid me to complete my purchase of my very first commercial property in the US.

Moving into the new building after months of renovation was not an easy task. We had the accumulation of more than ten years of inventories and buying and selling. It took weeks to get everything moved out and to start our business at the new store, the new location. And in this very location, in this very building, we began to enjoy ownership of property and never having to worry about the landlord, about the rent being doubled, or even possibly tripled, for that matter. This line of poetry once inspired me, and I cannot help but to quote here. It says:

ZZZZZ

"You brought me to the cliff
You pushed me off the edge
And I ... soared."

ZZZZZ

Years have gone by, and our lives have been blessed with four beautiful grandchildren: three granddaughters, Camranh Madison Le, from Tuan and Tina, and Chelsea Lien Le and Kyah Ann Le, and a grandson, Brady Bao Le, from Lam and Laurie.

One day early in December of last year, a customer came to

the store to look for furniture to buy. After a couple of visits, he came to me and said, more of statement than a question, "You are Vietnamese? I was in Vietnam in the sixties."

Once in a while I have been asked this type of question by some of the Vietnam vets in town who came to visit at the store, and I felt very connected with those who asked. We would normally go into conversations of the location where he had been stationed and length of time of his stay in my country. In this particular case, when I asked him what branch of service that he had served in during his tour of duty in Vietnam, his answer drew my deep interest and gave me a sense of camaraderie immediately. He said he had served in the Special Forces group airborne.

"Special Forces? You were in the Special Forces? Where at? Under whose command?" was a series of questions I posed to him without giving him time to answer. Anyhow, he said he was assigned to the Special Forces but was not SF himself. I told him the story of my former commander of A team, captain Ray Striler, who had saved my life by sending me off to a B team, headquarter in the heart of the city of Ban Me Thuot that ran all A teams. My replacement had been killed only a few weeks after my departure, and I had been looking for Captain Striler's whereabouts ever since the war was over, especially since I came to the United States.

Moved by my short story, perhaps by my personal experience of the war in which he was fighting on my behalf, he offered his help to find Ray for me.

John Miller was his name; he was a building contractor in town. He gave me his business card, and with an affirmative tone of voice, he told me, "I will find him for you."

"But how?" I then asked.

"I have my ways; don't you worry. I will let you know," John assured me.

I told him that we were going to close the store for Christmas break and that we were going to head out to Mount Hood, Oregon, where Lam had rented a vacation home at the ski resort. We would be back in Spokane for business the day after Christmas.

We exchanged our Christmas wishes and parted our ways.

It was the last night of our gathering at the Mount Hood retreat house, where our kids and their families joined us for the pre-holiday celebration. Right after dinner, when the dishes were still on the table, Lam asked me, "Dad, how did you get your name Sam? Your real name is Lien, right?" It was a very legitimate question, for none of my family members knew the story behind it. No one had ever asked about my nickname, and here it came from the curious mind of my son. It was perfect timing for this type of question, especially in the family setting. It was cold and snowing outside. The fireplace was glowing, with firewood cracking its way into the flames, giving away a little unescaped smoke over the room along with a faint but exquisite smell of cedar. I knew all the eyes and attention were on me, waiting for the story of my name, Sam.

It went back to the sixties, I told my audience, when I was under the command of Captain Ray Striler, who was a tall and handsome Green Beret officer. Somehow he had sent my picture back to his friends and girlfriend in the US, without letting me know. Then one day, out of the blue, a very thick, fat letter came addressed to me in care of Commander Capt. Striler. I was both very curious and happy to have a letter from the US. Curious because I did not recognize the sender, Harriet Hillman, from New Jersey; I had never heard or known of the name. I was happy because it was from the United States of America, whose soldiers were with me here in my homeland, fighting for a very common cause.

In the letter, or the contents of the letter, I told my family audience, was a picture of Harriet Hillman, a blond, good-looking girl who said lots of things, but at the very end of it, she said, "You are so very cute. I am going to call you Sam; there is no meaning to it, but it is cute." And I was nicknamed Sam ever since.

My kid audience, out of their youthful imagination and playfulness, did not accept that seemingly simple explanation of the letter. They asked me, "Are you sure there was nothing else to it besides she nicknamed you?"

I laughed myself away from that lovingly teasing accusation.

Then I went on to tell them about the incident in which Capt. Striler decided to ship me off to B team headquarters after our camp was attacked with artillery rounds from the enemy. Two weeks after my departure, my replacement was killed with a single sniper shot to his forehead that instantly took his life.

I could hear the sound of water running in the river outside the house, for my audience and the whole space deepened with the silence at the twist of fate in my life story.

Lam broke the silence again with his own insight, saying, "So if Ray had not made that decision to send you off to the B team, then there would not be mom, there would not be me or Tuan or Jonathan, and there would not be … all here."

"That is right," I said to him, "and that is my miracle of life," I added. Everything happened for a reason, whether you understand it or not.

It was just so interesting that things happened in my life thirty or forty years ago that I had never had time, never had the chance, to share with my kids. Here they were asking me in such an insightful way to tell them my own stories. I felt so good about sharing with them, especially in this environment by the fireplace at the end of the year. Outside the house, through the all-glass window facing the river, the white snow, like thread of cotton flakes, was quietly coming down into the night.

The holidays were over; we were all back to work. Snow continued to fill the ground of Spokane with many more inches each day. It was the morning of December 27, 2007. Lam called me from the store. "Dad, John Miller is here to see you."

"Who is John Miller?" I asked. I had forgotten who he was; my poor short memory!

"Well, why don't you just come over, he's waiting for you," he said.

"I will be on my way," I told Lam before I hung up.

The snow was coming down with thick flakes, and the road was a bit icy. As soon as I parked my car in front of the store, I spotted John Miller inside the front doors, and then I remembered he had promised me that he would find Ray just a few weeks ago. I immediately felt a sense of urgency because something had encouraged him to come to visit me at this time of the day under these weather conditions. Once I was inside the door and greeted him, he showed me two pieces of paper. One displayed a picture of tall handsome Ray in black pajamas, which was the uniform for us in the special clandestine operations then, and the other showed the two e-mails exchanged between Ray and John.

"Is it he?" John asked me as he was watching me at last.

I could not believe my eyes. It took me a few seconds into my memory bank, and *click!* "Yes, John," I told him as I was holding the picture, and I forgot the time had passed since I last saw him at Tan Rai camp. He must have had this picture taken at the time I was at the camp with him, and yes, he was the one I had been looking for so many years. I glanced at the e-mail he wrote to John, identifying himself as CO at Tan Rai A-232, now retired as a Lieutenant Colonel. His e-mail address was included, and best of all, his phone number was there.

I told John how much I appreciated his efforts to find Ray for me. I was very grateful to him. I told him that I was going to call Ray right away and keep him posted of what was going to happen next.

"Good luck, Sam," John said to me as he walked out the doors.

The phone was ringing on the other end after I punched in the number. Was I a bit nervous? Yes, I was! Would he still remember who I was? Would he recognize my voice? How would I address him? He was no longer in the military, so rank would not be appropriate; besides, he was retired as Lieutenant Colonel, as I noticed in his e-mail to John. Before I could settle for what it would be then, "Hello," he said over the phone.

"Is this Mr. Striler?" I decided to go with his last name.

"Yes, this is he," he said. At this I was trying to hold myself together.

"Sir," I said, "this is Sam under your command at Tan Rai camp back in the sixties."

I just could not finish what I intended to say to him, for I was trying to push, to hold my emotion down. I simply choked; my eyes were all welled up, and I became silent. He, at the other end of the line, was emotionally choked as well. It took us a long while before we could resume our conversation. He said he was driving to San Diego and would like to catch up with me later. I also asked if I could say hello to his wife, who was riding with him. Heidi, his wife, was very kind and sweet on the phone; we talked for a minute or so and promised that we would talk more later. I decided to let Ray fill her in with more information about me or about us.

While waiting for our next phone call in the evening, I let Lam know that I had just found Ray Striler, whom I mentioned at our gathering at the Mount Hood retreat house. He was very surprised at how things pulled together as if there had been some sort of collaboration by the divine, by the spirit. First, John Miller, who came in out of the blue, whom I had not known from Adam, came to offer me help. Next was the inquiry from Lam about my name at the dinner, which then led to the story I told my family. Now, after forty some plus years, each of us drifting away, being pulled into many different directions, I found Captain Striler here in the US. There was synchronicity at work, and miracles do happen!

The evening came, and the two of us were on the phone for hours catching up on the old days. I asked Ray what prompted his decision to ship me out of the war zone. His answer was that there was an intelligence report that I was on the list to be killed, and he told me that he did not want to go in too much detail on this over the phone. I told him about my going-through-hell stories after the war was over and brief stories of my escape from Vietnam to become one of the boat people.

I told him that I wanted to come down to see him and his family. He was very thrilled about that and said they lived in Carlsbad near San Diego in a small adobe house and wanted me to stay with them, even though the room in the attic was small. I told him he should not be concerned about that because after all, I was still a soldier in every noble sense, his soldier who could sleep on a floor with just a blanket. Ray laughed delightedly at the idea and said that he would not do that to me. While the idea of going to see him in Carlsbad flashed in my mind, I asked myself, "Why not ask him to come to Spokane to see me?" As my thoughts became words, I suggested that we all could celebrate our reunion, our losing and finding each other after almost half of a century. I told him that I would call all media stations in Spokane to tell them our story, the story of Captain Ray Striler, who, while serving in Vietnam as commanding officer of a special forces A team, had a big and kind heart to send me off to a safer place before the Communists could get their hands on me. I would have my family come with friends and admirers to meet him at the Spokane International Airport. He liked the idea but wanted to keep a low profile. After all, I just wanted to tell the whole world that he was my hero and I wanted to express my gratitude.

As our talk continued into the late evening, I found out that he had been back to Vietnam at least four times to work with schools to promote education in our postwar-torn country. That really impressed me even more, for it fit into what I have been doing for the children in Vietnam. I knew that education was the only remedy to heal this country and to bring a better life to all Vietnamese in the years to come, and I would continue to promote it at every chance that came.

We concluded our talk that evening with my final question for him: "Sir, how old are you now, may I ask?"

Ray stiffened and said, "I was born December 21, 193—"

Before he could finish, I butted in. "I was also born on December 21." We both hesitated for a moment as that sank in. Then I understood many things all at once; I could see why we were so close in thought and deed. He went on to say, "—1938" and added, "Sam, you were twenty years old during that time at Tan Rai, and I was the old man at twenty-seven years. Go figure."

I gasped to myself as I was mentally figuring out his age. With an accepting smile, Ray said, "Sam, you are my younger brother." I cried with joy.

The year was coming to an end with a happy note for me, for I had found Ray, a soldier who saved my life and changed my destiny. He was a hero and now my big brother.